free-motion QUILTING

from Ordinary
to Extraordinary

3 Steps to Joyful Machine Stitching in 21 Days

Jenny K. Lyon

C&T PUBLISHING

Text copyright © 2018 by Jenny K. Lyon
Photography and artwork copyright © 2018 by C&T Publishing, Inc.

Publisher: Amy Marson
Creative Director: Gailen Runge
Acquisitions Editor: Roxane Cerda
Managing Editor: Liz Aneloski
Editor: Christine Doyle
Technical Editor: Debbie Rodgers
Cover/Book Designer: April Mostek
Production Coordinator: Tim Manibusan
Production Editor: Alice Mace Nakanishi
Illustrator: Linda Johnson
Photo Assistant: Mai Yong Vang

Quilt photography by Lucy Glover and instructional photography by Mai Yong Vang of C&T Publishing, Inc., unless otherwise noted

Published by C&T Publishing, Inc., P.O. Box 1456, Lafayette, CA 94549

Library of Congress Cataloging-in-Publication Data
Names: Lyon, Jenny K., 1954- author.
Title: Free-motion quilting from ordinary to extraordinary : 3 steps to joyful machine stitching in 21 days / Jenny K. Lyon.
Description: Lafayette, CA : C&T Publishing, Inc., 2018.
Identifiers: LCCN 2018005042 | ISBN 9781617456374 (soft cover)
Subjects: LCSH: Patchwork--Patterns. | Machine quilting--Patterns.
Classification: LCC TT835 .L945 2018 | DDC 746.44/5041--dc23
LC record available at https://lccn.loc.gov/2018005042

Printed in the USA
10 9 8 7 6 5 4 3 2 1

ACKNOWLEDGMENTS

Quilting is a contact sport; we all need each other. I am grateful to all of the following:

My students: You are my passion and joy. I learn so much from you.

My local quilt guild, the Folsom Quilt and Fiber Guild: You got me started and keep me going.

Studio Art Quilt Associates: You inspire and challenge me and have given me friendships around the world.

American Sewing Guild, Gold Country Chapter: Your friendships will last a lifetime.

Afro-American Quilters of Los Angeles: Your creativity, enthusiasm, and willingness to share were an encouragement to me.

SIS: My home small group. I know I can land here, be supported and understood.

Nancy Burnett, Helen Hardwick, and Laura Rylander: Your friendship and support has been invaluable to me.

Meissner Sewing Center: You encouraged me to teach and continue to support my passion to teach.

Diane Gaudynski, the best teacher, artist, and quilter ever: You continue to amaze me.

Cate Coulocos Prato: For your timely help and superb editing skills.

C&T Publishing: For encouraging and supporting this first-time author.

Franki Kohler and Barbara Hunter: For sharing your beautiful postcards.

Mom: You taught me that if I wanted it, I'd better figure out how to make it. Best. Advice. Ever.

Art Lyon: I couldn't do any of this without your love and understanding. Thank you for your unwavering confidence in me and for learning how to cook.

My God: Thank you for blessing me with a life and talent that can glorify You.

DEDICATION

To any quilter striving to find her or his own voice and become successful at free-motion quilting, this is for you. I *know* you can successfully free-motion quilt and enjoy it! I've got a plan for you—read on....

Contents

43

48

53

57

62

Note: It's not practice, it's play! Let's "**plactice**"!

Personal Note

I was given a needle at age six and taught how to use it by my mother. As a child I dabbled in all manner of handwork. I was ecstatic when it was determined I was old enough to sew on a machine! I sewed the typical garments of the day: dirndl skirts, shifts, and aprons. My ultimate project was a fully tailored polyester pantsuit.

Photo by Jenny K. Lyon

A few of my mother's quilts displayed at her funeral—she was prolific!

My mother made quilt tops and sent them out to Amish women for hand quilting. I was not particularly interested in quilting as a child, but I did learn an important lesson from my mother: If you want it, you'd better figure out how to make it yourself.

I made my first quilt in the mid-1980s with the resurgence of the craft. Although I was excited about quilting, motherhood took over for the next fifteen years. I made my first machine-quilted quilt in 1999, and I haven't stopped!

I then completed several quilts in a short period, yet I was still afraid to quilt my own "important" quilts. I knew I was competent at free-motion quilting, but I wasn't quite ready to do the kind of work I yearned to do. How was I going to get to the point where I was joyfully and confidently quilting my own work?

I took classes to improve my skills and I learned from each. I learned the technical aspects, yes, but more importantly I learned to be *fearless*. I gained confidence and was no longer paralyzed by my mistakes—I learned that even the pros made mistakes.

In 2006, I made what I felt was a breakthrough quilt, *If Diane Met Karen* (page 75). Its design was an original wholecloth quilt, made entirely of luscious silk. It greatly exceeded my expectations, and I was proud and excited!

While I was quilting that project, I had to force myself to take breaks. I was so excited about what was coming from my needle that I would skip around the house in joy during my breaks. That is when I decided I was a "quilt skipper"—and that became the name of my blog years later.

It is my hope that each of my students has a "quilt skipping" moment, a moment in time when you are in awe of what you are creating and it excites you to the core of your soul. Now *that* is what motivates me to travel and teach!

Introduction

> I've written this book for the free-motion quilter who is at a crossroads. Maybe you've taken a few classes, limped through a few projects, or even quilted a few quilts. But you're frustrated. You want to confidently quilt all those fabulous tops in your stash, but you're afraid. You're not ready to quilt your "special" quilts.

I know that anyone who wants to free-motion quilt *can* do it, but how do you become a joyful and confident free-motion quilter?

Start your journey with **Inspiration** (page 7) and learn how to find and collect images that inspire *you*. Use that base to create your own motifs to put on your quilts to make them more meaningful.

Then, in **Before You Take a Stitch** (page 14), take an in-depth look at the decisions you make—on batting, fabric, needles, tension, thread—that significantly affect the quilting process and your quilting experience.

At the heart of this book is a three-step plan to show you how to bridge the gap between ordinary and extraordinary free-motion quilting, without endless and boring practice.

In **Step 1: 21 Days of "Plactice"** (page 30), I present a roadmap to build up your confidence and skills.

Note: It's not practice, it's play! Let's "**plactice**"!

In Week 1 of the 21 days, you will build your motif inventory. The simple process of free-motion quilting for twenty minutes a day and playing with new motifs will quickly give you new ideas for your quilting. I've included an **Appendix of Quilting Motifs** (page 92) to get you started. This is the week to experiment and discover what you enjoy and what challenges you. Play around with free-motion stitching without pressure.

In Week 2, you will learn to combine the motifs you know to create new designs, create new motifs from objects in your everyday life, and find new motifs from the work of others. New motifs are out there for you to discover and add to your own work. Having a larger inventory of motifs makes quilting more fun and personal.

In Week 3, it's time to start putting all those new skills to use on small items. I've included a variety of playful ideas for items that can be completed quickly. Try one or two and begin to feel the joy of creating quilted items for the home, yourself, or others. Each is small enough to experiment on without stress.

In **Step 2: Five to Learn On** (page 42), you'll learn approachable and fun projects that prepare you to move on to more challenging quilts.

> **Choose the one(s) that appeal to you the most.**
>
> • Fabric Postcards (page 43) can be completed in an afternoon and are a great small format to highlight your new skills.
>
> • Panel Quilts (page 48), from preprinted panels, are the perfect place to try new techniques before committing to them on a major quilt.
>
> • Quilt-from-the-Back Quilt (page 53) teaches a technique to get impressive quilting by following the lines of a large-scale print fabric.
>
> • Quilt-as-You-Go Quilt (page 57) shows how to quilt large quilts on your home machine easily by using the split batting method.
>
> • Boho Cutwork Denim Jacket (page 62) uses a simple cutwork technique on your own purchased jacket to achieve stunning results.

In **Step 3: Your Personal Quilting World** (page 70), learn to create a quilting world to suit *just you*, including the types of quilting you are passionate about. I encourage you to show others the beautiful quilts you have made and to join a group with like-minded quilters.

I've also included my own **Gallery of Quilts** (page 75) to show my journey from traditional quilts to the whole-cloth quilts I make today. I share some of my triumphs and challenges along the way.

This book will help you confidently quilt the projects you long to quilt, whether you are a traditional, modern, art, or any other kind of quilter.

You *can* quilt those "special" quilts; you can even enter your quilts in shows if that's your thing. With a little play and a plan, you *can* be the rock star quilter you want to be (see Now Quilt That Quilt!, page 91).

A NOTE ON BEING FEARLESS

It is my hope that you will approach your free-motion quilting with gusto and confidence. No matter what your skill set, be fearless!

Many of my students begin class with fear and end up full of hope. What builds up that hope in such a short period? Practicing free-motion quilting in a supportive and encouraging atmosphere.

I know that anyone can free-motion quilt with skill and confidence. Fear is what holds us back. Think about it: What is there to be afraid of? No one will be harmed if your free-motion quilting is not fabulous. Nations will not fall; war will not break out.

What happens if you *pretend* to be fearless, even if you don't feel it at first? You will persevere and create your own confidence. Nothing will keep you from tackling that next project. Keep quilting—you *will* get better!

Inspiration

Every quilt grows from a seed of inspiration. Whether your quilt is made from a kit or from an original design, something inspired you.

All quilters are motivated by inspiration, so don't think inspiration is just for "artists"! After all, inspiration is simply your own collection of ideas that got your attention and made your heart sing.

Mossy stacked stone wall

Finding Inspiration

Creativity flows from careful observation of life's details. Focus on seeing your world more mindfully. There is form, line, color, shape, and texture in *every* scene. Even mundane, everyday items—such as company logos, advertisements, or even tissue boxes—can include inspirational motifs. Just remember to be mindful of any copyright issues. If in doubt, ask permission or don't use it.

INSPIRATION CHALLENGE

Challenge yourself to find inspiration in your everyday world:

- Grasses
- Shadows
- Bumpers of cars
- Details from your daily walks
- Unscripted scenes of people interacting

Most of my personal inspiration comes from my own yard, from nature in general, or from childhood memories.

This image inspired *Oat Grass* (page 82).

Author's backyard

Photos on this page by Jenny K. Lyon

I am so fortunate to have a fabulous yard. When I moved to northern California from the East Coast, I was smitten by the drought-tolerant landscapes here—I had never seen such a thing before! The colors were more subdued, but the texture and movement was glorious!

My yard is a source of constant beauty and inspiration. With the slightest of breezes, my grasses will bob and wave.

Succulents of many forms and colors, some with outrageously colorful blooms, gather in sunny spots. It is a joy to walk my plot; it changes daily with sun, shadow, breeze, and season.

Look at the texture of this bark!

These scenes from my yard and life have provided endless inspiration for subject matter, quilting motifs, and color stories.

Gaura flower in the spring

Author as a little girl

Memories also provide inspiration. The vivid recollection of a favorite flowerbed next to my childhood home inspired *Mom's Lily Bed* (page 78). Images of magnificent fall weather while living in northern New Jersey inspired *Golden Moments* (page 76). A singular memory of a dress I wore in first grade provides the inspiration for my work with sheer fabric.

Lily-of-the-valley

That's me. What inspires you?

Collecting Images

The inspiration process is about collecting the images, feelings, scenes, and colors that excite you and putting them into an accessible format. My advice: Keep it simple.

There are so many ways of collecting what inspires you: Keep them in a sketchbook or on your camera, make physical copies, use online methods like Pinterest and apps, or take notes on your phone. Accumulate those images without editing; you saw something that piqued your interest, so hang onto it!

I don't have a complex method for keeping images. I have a Pinterest account and also keep physical copies of some images. I organize them in a format that works for me: simple paper folders.

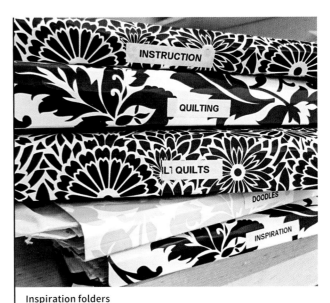
Inspiration folders

Glorious zinnia

Photos on these facing pages by Jenny K. Lyon

When my creative well is running dry, I return to those humble folders and cull from my Pinterest pages to find inspiration.

As time passes and your inspirational folders and sketchbooks grow, review each on occasion. Which ideas excite you the most right now?

Airport reflections

Ivy on the wall

Your focus and tastes will change over time, and you'll find different ideas coming to the surface each time you review your images. I take my "images du jour" and work from them for my current inspiration.

Creating Your Own Free-Motion Fills and Motifs

So you've accumulated a collection of inspiring images that you'd like to include in your own work. How can you incorporate that inspiration into your quilts? A quilt becomes personal when you include fills and motifs that you have designed yourself. I treasure the quilts that include my own fills and motifs—they make my quilts unique.

You may feel unequipped to design your own filler combinations, but with a little time and sketching, you can do it. Start with pencil sketches and try combining different motifs.

SKETCHING WITH WHITE PEN

Try sketching with a white pen on black paper. The unexpected use of white on black can trick your mind and create fresh, new motifs. I don't exactly know how, but it works!

The process of designing your own motifs may not be a direct step-by-step process.

If you want to make a free-motion quilting motif, use these ideas as starting points.

- Simplify a motif you'd like to use. For *Mom's Lily Bed* (page 78), the lily-of-the-valley was key to the quilt. But the lily is a complex flower. I decided to simplify it, making the flower a simple circle. The beauty of the design became the curved stem and successively smaller circles.

- Start with a motif you know and alter it: Try echoing it, altering the shape, altering the scale, or adding embellishments (see Echoed Ribbon Border, page 93).

- Combine two or more motifs into a fill. Experiment with motifs you know and see if you can combine them. I combined a simple S-curve, repeated it, and added Half-Moons (page 92) to create Flutter (page 93). Similarly I combined Daisies (page 92) and Bubbles (page 92) in the design for Boho Cutwork Denim Jacket (page 62).

Photos on this page by Jenny K. Lyon

Here are a few basic principles and tips to get you started designing your own free-motion motifs.

1. Consider the space you want to fill. Do you envision a single design or several? Smaller spaces can each be happy with a single design. Larger spaces need a little more thought. Combining several fills can create delightful texture without detracting from the design focus. If you choose to combine motifs in a large area, consider using motifs that are easiest for you. Why make it difficult?

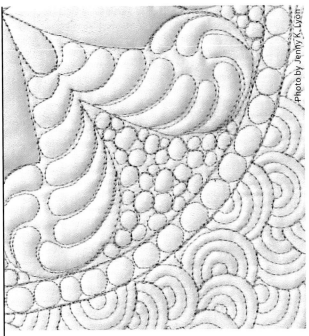

A motif and a fill were all that were needed to fill this small inner circle.

Here I combined a variety of motifs that were repeated throughout the panel.

2. Consider the type of quilting that's best for that area. Adding linear or grid-based motifs somewhere on the quilt gives the eye a place to rest. If the area adjoins a curve, it can be stunning to put a grid next to the curve, so each motif enhances the other.

Trapunto class sample with radiating lines

3. Consider the density of the quilting. Densely quilted designs compress the background and highlight the areas they surround.

Detail of *Mom's Lily Bed* (page 78)

4. Consider the scale of your motifs. A large-scale fill can compete with a featured motif. By scaling down a fill, the feature motif will stand out more.

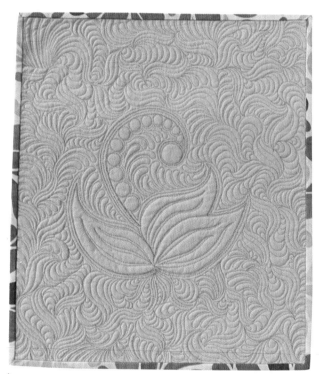

The outside fill competes with the central motif because the scale of both is similar.

5. Consider unity. Repeating fills throughout your quilt creates unity. When repeating a motif, sometimes you will need to quilt over a previously quilted line to get where you need to go. Doubling over the lines is okay! If you are stumped on how to make a singular motif into a fill, think about traveling over previously quilted lines to allow for the repeat.

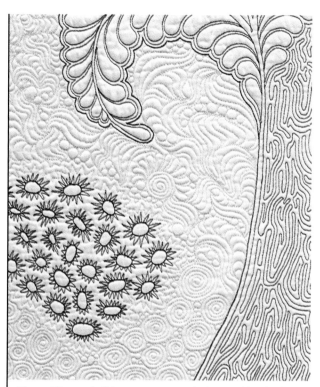

The motifs seen in this area were repeated across *Morning Breeze* (next page and page 80).

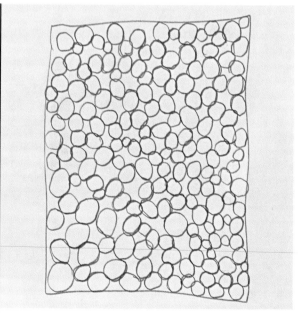

It's impossible to do pebbles without traveling over previously quilted lines.

You might be surprised by how quickly you create your own usable and personal motifs. Persevere until you find your own designs that sing!

Mission Statement

Once I have used my inspiration images to create a plan for my quilt, I create a mission statement. It might sound odd, but I create a mission statement for all my major quilts. A mission statement merely captures the vision and inspiration I have for that quilt in a sentence or two.

My statement gives me something to refer back to as I make design decisions or when I get stuck or feel overwhelmed. It's a bumper that keeps me on course. I do give myself permission to thoughtfully change my mission statement as I go if I choose a different path.

As an example, my mission statement for *Morning Breeze* was "To capture the feeling of movement and the joy I feel on my morning walks." Keeping track of the end goal is especially encouraging when I feel like I will never finish!

Photo by RCP Scanning Services

Morning Breeze

Before You Take a Stitch

Envision that you are ready to begin quilting one of your special quilts. It is pieced, basted, and marked. The quilt is in your machine, under the needle, and you are ready to take your first stitch.

Freeze frame! Whether you realize it or not, you have already made many decisions that will affect how easy or difficult it is to quilt that quilt. In this chapter, I take a closer look at those choices and help you make the best decisions for your machine, your quilting area, and your quilt.

Your Machine and Quilting Area

Choosing a Machine

You want to love your machine! A great machine need not be expensive or new. Whatever machine you have, you want it to sew like a dream. It should be able to handle the thick and thin of what you sew, the foot control should be easy to modulate, and it should have the features you want, which may include speed control, needle-up/down, self-threading, larger throat, and preprogrammed stitches.

If you decide that you need a new or different machine, I have a few suggestions to make the process less confusing.

SET A BUDGET

You do not want to get excited about a machine that exceeds your budget! You may want to consider the cost of a cabinet in your budget, too. It's much easier to quilt or sew with your machine set into a cabinet. Also, there may be feet or accessories that you may want or need, such as a walking foot, a zipper foot, or a tote to haul your machine.

If the machine you desire is outside of your budget, consider buying a used machine. Most dealers have a selection of quality used machines from customers who have traded up.

KNOW YOUR NEEDS

There are all kinds of sewing machines on the market today. Buy a machine that fits *your* needs. For example, I don't machine embroider, so I don't need to spend extra money on embroidery capabilities.

You may see yourself "growing" into other types of sewing. I advise waiting until you are ready to try something new before upgrading your machine. Buy a machine made for the kind of sewing you do now.

CABINET ALTERNATIVE

If you cannot afford a cabinet for your machine, consider a sturdy portable table. A portable sewing table allows you to set your machine flush with the table surface for much less than a full cabinet.

LIGHTWEIGHT MACHINES

Lightweight machines are scaled down in size and have fewer features. However, I have seen some amazing quilting and sewing come from them! If this is to be your primary machine, make sure you are comfortable quilting and sewing on a smaller machine with fewer features.

WHERE TO BUY

Where you buy your machine makes a difference! You are purchasing more than a machine—you're buying service and support.

> Your local independent sewing machine dealer has some notable advantages over online or big box stores.

- Their staff is educated on your brand of machine and can help solve problems.

- They usually offer machine maintenance, which you will need at least once a year.

- Most dealerships offer lessons to go with the machine and *you need those lessons*!

- Many dealerships also offer quality fabric and thread and know their merchandise well.

- Most will match pricing from other sources or offer financing.

TAKE YOUR TIME

Take your time choosing a machine. You want to clearly understand the differences, advantages, and disadvantages between the models and brands.

The bottom line is this: Take the time to make a confident selection so that you go home with a machine you absolutely love!

Machine Set-Up

Before you begin to free-motion quilt, you'll want to create the best set-up possible for your machine.

STRAIGHT-STITCH PLATE

I recommend a straight-stitch plate for free-motion quilting. A zigzag plate came with your machine; you may have to purchase a straight-stitch plate. The needle hole on a straight-stitch plate is smaller and holds the fabric more firmly, resulting in a slightly better free-motion stitch.

Most machines do not come with a straight-stitch plate; it is an additional purchase.

GRIP AND SLIP

It will be much easier to move your quilt and achieve beautiful, even stitches if you have something grippy on our hands and something slippery on the bed of the machine—"grip" and "slip."

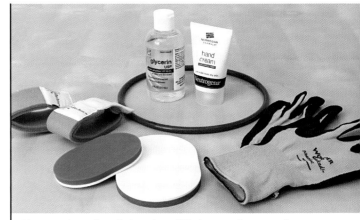

These are just a few choices that will help you grip your quilt.

There are many ways to add grip to your hands so that you can move the quilt easily. Choosing the right gripping aide is a personal decision. I prefer to wear quilting gloves, but you may prefer a hoop, disks, bands, lotion or glycerin. Experiment with different methods to choose the one that works best for you.

The less friction between the quilt and sewing surface, the easier it will be to free-motion quilt. I recommend adding a Teflon slider to the bed of the machine for zero friction. Simply smooth the slider out over the bed of the machine, with the cutout resting under the needle.

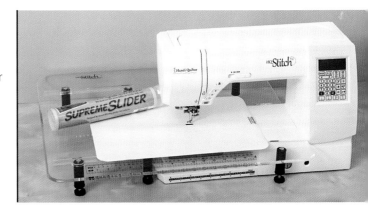

CARE OF YOUR SLIDER

A slider needs to be kept clean, or it will move and you'll quilt through it and ruin it. To clean off bits of fiber, periodically take the slider to a sink, run water over the back, and the fiber bits will release. Give it a few shakes and place it back onto the machine bed.

Needles

TYPES OF NEEDLES

Opinions abound about the best needles to use for free motion. I recommend two types of needles for most free-motion quilting: a sharps needle or a topstitch needle.

Sharps The sharps needle (called a microtex needle in the Schmetz brand) is great when using thin threads (80- or 100-weight). It leaves a small hole behind, allowing the sheen of the thread to show through. A sharps needle is also useful for tightly woven fabrics like batiks and for wholecloth quilts.

Topstitch For most other applications, I use a topstitch needle. The topstitch needle has a large eye and deep groove. Its sturdy design and point allow it to penetrate multiple layers of fabric, like where seams meet on a quilt top.

Topstitch needles with titanium or chrome plating are a bit more expensive, but the coating allows the needle to last significantly longer than steel needles.

CHANGING NEEDLES

No matter the type of needle you use, it is important to change it as soon as it gets dull. A dull needle can damage fabric, leaving pulled threads in its wake.

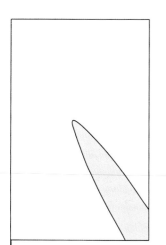

A dull needle may seem fine, but if you could magnify it, you'd see that the point is actually flattened. You wouldn't want to quilt with this!

Do you know how to tell if your needle is dull?

1. Listen. You will hear a popping sound from the needle breaking threads as it enters the fabric.

2. Look. The visible signs of a dull needle include shredded or broken thread, pulled fabric threads, and skipped stitches.

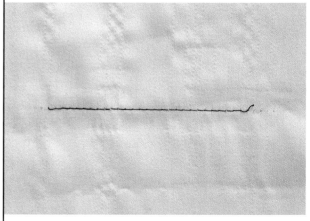

Fabric damaged by a dull needle

NEEDLE SIZE

Needle size will vary depending on the thickness of the thread you choose.

There are too many threads to list what each would pair with, but these are the general guidelines I follow:

- Size 9/70 or 7/60 is best for 80- to 100-weight threads.
- Size 11/80 is best for mid-range threads, 50- to 60-weight.
- Size 14/90 is best for heavier threads, 30- or 40-weight.
- Size 16/100 or above is best for specialty heavyweight threads.

Some thread manufacturers stamp the suggested needle size on the spool. Signs that you have the wrong size needle include broken or frayed thread or irregular stitches.

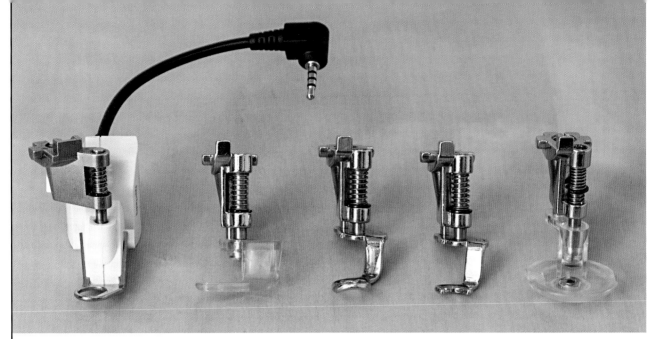

You have choices on feet; choose the best one for your machine.

Machine Feet

Your machine may have several choices in a free-motion foot. The best foot will provide maximum visibility of both the needle hitting the fabric and your quilting.

Consider the following when choosing a foot:

- Feet with a cutout in the front provide better visibility of the needle.

- The shaft on a metal foot is usually thinner than on a plastic foot. This means a metal foot will give you a better view of completed stitches behind the foot.

Photo by Jenny K. Lyon

A *closed-toe* plastic foot may obscure where the needle hits as well as the stitching behind the needle.

Photo by Jenny K. Lyon

An *open-toe* metal foot gives a better view of where the needle hits and of the stitches behind the needle.

If you chose the foot with the best visibility, it will be easier to quilt well. I have seen a student's work instantly elevated after changing to a better foot. Work with your machine's dealer to find the best foot for your free-motion quilting. It is well worth the investment!

Quilting Area Set-Up

Consider the physical set-up of your quilting area. If it's uncomfortable to quilt, you won't enjoy it! You'll be amazed at how much more pleasant it is to quilt with well thought-out lighting and ergonomics.

LIGHTING

If you can't see your work well, you can't quilt well. Lighting is often overlooked, yet it is an important part of your set-up. The appropriate lighting will not just help you see what you're quilting, but it will prevent eyestrain and a sore neck and back. If you are slumped over trying to see, quilting will hurt!

When the lighting is inadequate, you will find yourself sitting hunched over.

With abundant lighting, you'll be able to sit upright and comfortably.

A combination of overhead and task lighting works best. First consider the light on your machine. Machines vary in the quality of the light they provide. Machines with longer harps usually have excellent lighting due to the addition of lighting in the harp area.

If the machine does not have lighting in the harp area, consider an add-on light. Your choices include stick-on lights with a separate electrical cord; lights that use either a USB port or plug-in power; or a gooseneck light that sticks onto the machine to the left of the needle

A good floor lamp lets you clearly see what you've just quilted.

It is also helpful to have additional lighting for the back side of the machine so you can see what you've just quilted. A floor lamp is a welcome addition.

I have found the addition of a magnifying lamp essential. It provides an abundance of light wherever it's needed and the magnification allows detailed work to be quilted with ease.

Finally, you will also need excellent overhead lighting in your quilting area.

It's so much more pleasant to quilt when a sewing area is well lighted. You want a sewing and quilting area to be the most pleasant place in your home. No more hunched-back quilting!

A clamp-on magnifier adds light and magnification exactly where you need it. Once you have this type of light, you will never want to be without it.

Photos on this page by Jenny K. Lyon

MACHINE AND TABLE

Ideally your machine is set flush with the top of the table or a well-made, sturdy portable table. If possible, avoid having the machine set up on a table surface. It makes it more difficult to quilt with the machine sitting so high.

If the machine does set up on a table, an acrylic surround table is a useful addition. The additional surround makes for easier maneuvering of the quilt.

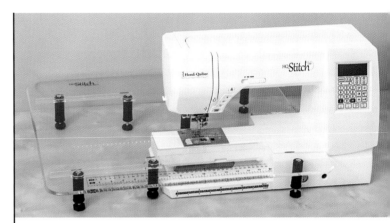

It is much easier to quilt when the quilt and the table are all at same level.

Acrylic surrounds are great to have on retreats or for class.

SURROUND

You'll need plenty of room to the left and back of the machine to carry the weight and bulk of your quilt and to keep it from falling off the table. You cannot quilt well if you are fighting the weight of the quilt.

If the machine's table does not have enough area around the machine, surround it with other tables such as card tables, console tables, or even an ironing board.

Since the bulk of the quilt will always be to the left of the machine, placing a small table there will keep the quilt from falling off the front of the machine's table.

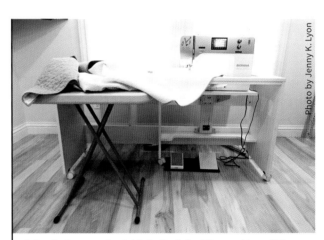

A simple, inexpensive table to the left of the machine will keep the quilt from falling to the floor.

A table with room to accommodate the bulk and weight of the quilt is useful.

Photo by koalastudios.com. Used with permission.

CHAIR

You'll want the most comfortable chair you can afford, one that adjusts up and down with a seat wide enough to be comfortable. Whether it has arms or not is a personal decision.

CHOOSING A CHAIR

Your chair should be comfortable to *sew* in, so test chairs based on your sewing position, which is more forward in the chair.

FOOT CONTROL

The foot control should be placed so that your knee is at a 90° angle and your body remains square to the machine. You don't want to stretch to reach the foot control—that would be uncomfortable.

BODY PLACEMENT

Place yourself so that your nose is aligned with the needle, your body square to the machine at the shoulders and hips, and your elbows close to your body. Position your chair so that the angle of your elbows and knees is a little greater than 90°. Experiment and find the most comfortable position.

All this positioning can make a huge difference in your quilting experience. Be kind to yourself and adjust to a comfortable position.

A chair made for sewing is comfortable to sit in for long periods.

You're more comfortable if your hips and shoulders are square to the machine.

Photos on this page by Jenny K. Lyon

Your Quilt

Once you have your machine set up for function, ease, and comfort, it's time to think about the many choices you make that affect the quilt. Making mindful decisions about thread, fabric, basting, and marking can make your quilting experience more comfortable, successful, and pleasant.

Fabric

Quality fabric makes a difference! Low-quality fabric can lose its color, disintegrate before the other higher quality fabrics in a quilt, and make an otherwise good quilt look terrible.

I made a quilt for my son in my early quilting years and used some low-quality fabrics. I was so disappointed to see some fabrics begin to disintegrate after just eighteen months of use!

I was part of an online challenge where we were to "doodle" in thread on a square of fabric. I was happy with my doodle, except the part that had the "straight lines"— they were quite wobbly! Ultimately I figured out that the problem was my fabric: It was so coarsely woven that it made my "straight" lines wobbly! Using the same needle, thread, and batting, but with quality fabric, my quilting looked much better.

Choose fabric wisely. Start with a quality store that knows their stock and buys premium fabrics. It has been rare for me to have a problem with fabric bought at my local quilt shop. If you begin to work with nonquilt fabrics, make sure you test by treating them as you will the quilt, essentially wash, iron, and tumble dry.

As to prewashing or not, I admit I am too impatient to prewash, and I have not had any significant issues as a result. However, it would be wise to prewash so there are no unpleasant surprises.

This piece was made for an online challenge. I was happy with my quilting except in the area of the parallel lines.

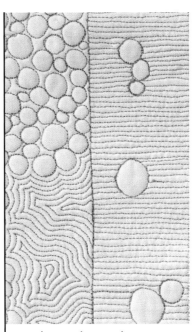

I used coarse, inexpensive fabric for my doodle. Note how my "straight" lines almost appear to be zigzag.

Quality fabric makes the quilting look better.

Thread

Thread choice is one of the most visible decisions. You probably already have some thread preferences. This overview of thread will help you understand the choices available and to make a decision that you are happy with.

THREAD CONTENT

When free-motion quilting, you can use almost any type of thread available on the market: cotton, polyester, monofilament (clear), silk, and metallic. But your choice should be compatible with the end use of the quilt. For example, I would not choose silk or metallic thread for a bed quilt because these threads could disintegrate with frequent washings and heavy use.

Also, thread types can be combined top and bobbin if you choose: cotton-wrapped polyester in the top with monofilament or silk in the bobbin, for example, or metallic in the top and cotton in the bobbin. I use cotton in the top and bobbin for piecing, but when free-motion quilting, I often combine thread types.

You may consider combining thread types for several reasons:

- You will get more thread per bobbin if you choose a thinner thread for the bobbin.

- If you use a slippery thread on top (metallic or poly-ester), consider a "grabbier" thread like cotton in the bobbin. Tension may be easier to adjust and retain.

- Using a different thread type in the bobbin may be a look that you like. In my black-and-white grass series, I used silk thread in the bobbin. I love the sheen that it gives to the back!

You may prefer to match threads in the top and bobbin, and that is fine, too. Just know that you have permission to play with different fibers when you're free-motion quilting.

THREAD QUALITY

Always use quality thread—the machine can tell the difference. Low-quality thread will give you fits as it shreds, breaks, and knots. A low-quality cotton thread will leave a trail of lint behind, possibly causing tension problems and, eventually, an expensive trip for service.

BUYING QUALITY THREAD

Buying a quality thread on sale is a good value. Buying inferior thread for any price is unwise.

To tell if your cotton thread is of high quality, try the break test. Take a 2- to 3-foot section of the thread, hold it firmly, and pull until it breaks. Quality cotton thread will snap; lower quality thread will fray or break unevenly.

Also, look for extralong staple cotton. Medium and short staple thread is weaker and lintier. If the label does not note the staple length, it is probably not extralong staple cotton.

To test the quality of polyester thread, unfurl several feet and hold taut between your hands. It should lie smooth, with no kinks or fuzz. Lower quality polyester thread will have small kinks and/or a rough cuticle. I quilted an entire quilt with low-quality polyester when I first started quilting. I almost gave up on quilting because it made ugly snags every few minutes, and I thought it was me!

Where you buy thread can make a difference in quality. In general, local quilt shops carry high-quality thread. The staff knows their thread lines well and can help you with your selection.

Start with quality thread.

THREAD WEIGHT

The thickness or weight of the thread you choose directly affects how it looks on the quilt. If you choose a thick thread, it will rest on top of the quilt and speak. If you choose a thinner thread, it will sink into the quilt, presenting line and shadow more than color—a whisper.

The choice of weight is a personal decision and one that might vary from project to project. The weight of the thread is expressed in a number. Generally, quilters are working with threads sized from a 12 (heavy) to 100 (thin).

THREAD WEIGHT NUMBERS

Think of thread weight numbers like this: It's the *opposite* of people weight. A high number is a skinny thread; a low number is a heavy thread.

Left feather: The very thin 100-weight silk thread sinks into the fabric, leaving line and shadow. *Right feather:* The 40-weight three-ply cotton thread is much thicker; it stands up on the surface of the quilt and makes a bolder statement.

THREAD PLY

Ply makes a difference, too. A thread's ply number is the number of yarns that are twisted together to make a single thread. It will be expressed as two numbers separated by a slash, such as 50/2. The first number indicates the weight of the thread, and the second indicates the number of plies that make that thread. Together, the ply and weight tell you how thick the thread is.

This may all be confusing, but don't fret. Over time you will know which threads work for you and your projects.

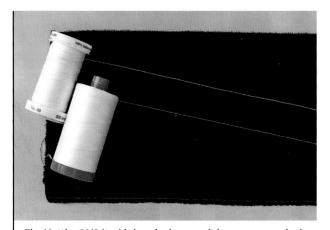

The Mettler 50/3 (*top*) is heavier because it has one more ply than the two-ply Aurifil 50/2 (*bottom*).

AUDITIONING THREAD

Keep yourself from having to rip out threads that don't work on your quilt by auditioning them first. These two steps will give you a very good idea of how that thread might look stitched out on your quilt.

1. Pull off enough thread to make a puddle. Pick up the thread puddle and move it around on the quilt to see how it looks on various parts of your quilt.

2. Pull off about 2 feet of thread and hold it taut between your hands. Place the thread on the quilt top in a variety of places to see how it looks.

A wide variety of batting is available. Be sure to match the end use of your quilt to the appropriate batting.

POLY

THERMORE

BAMBOO

SILK

WOOL

70/30

80/20

QLTRS DREAM REQUEST

QLTRS DREAM SELECT

WARM AND NATURAL

QLTRS DREAM ORIENT

WOOL BATTING

Wool batting is unique in free-motion quilting. It is extremely lightweight, shrinks very little, and compacts dramatically. This makes it easier to handle the bulk of a large quilt in a domestic machine.

However, it has significant loft, which can be tricky for a newer quilter. If you are mindful to raise the presser foot to barely skim the surface and securely baste, it becomes easier to quilt.

FOLD MARKS ON QUILTS

Ever notice that almost all antique quilts with cotton batting have a permanent fold mark? Animal fiber batting such as wool does not hold a fold. Plant fiber batting such as cotton will hold a fold. If you prefer to avoid fold marks, wool or silk batting would be a good choice.

Batting

Choose batting mindfully because it can make or break a quilt. Many quilters use the same batting for all projects, even though the end use of the projects varies. I recommend you consider stability, loft, fiber content, and end use for each quilt.

STABILITY

No matter the fiber content, all batting falls somewhere between sturdy and drapey. Each has its uses. For example, a sturdy batting is best for a table runner that you want to hold its shape. A drapey batting is a good choice for a child's quilt that will be cuddled.

LOFT

There are many choices in batting and their loft affects how easily each batting is quilted. In general, a thinner and/or lightweight batting is easier to quilt than a heavy batting.

FIBER CONTENT

Manufacturers are creating new blends to get the best qualities of each fiber. There are many varieties, each with its own unique properties. One of my favorite blends is Orient (by Quilters Dream), a blend of bamboo, silk, Tencel, and cotton. It is sturdy, lighter weight, and drapey—a great combination for a bed or cuddle quilt.

RECOMMENDATIONS

Below are useful tips, no matter what type of batting you choose.

- Buy the batting you want. The price difference between king-size 80/20 batting (80% cotton / 20% polyester) and king-size wool batting is $10–$20. Get the batting you love!

- Consider the loft and weight of the batting. A lighter, more compact batting is a good choice for large quilts that will be quilted on a domestic machine.

- Some batting is needle-punched and/or has added scrim. Both processes add stability to the batting. It's a personal choice whether you want the added stability or not.

- If you are working with a new-to-you batting, consider testing it first in a small wallhanging.

- Open up the batting and let it relax before basting the quilt. This will allow the wrinkles to fall out and basting will be easier.

Batting is an important choice and can significantly affect the ease of quilting, the final appearance, and the durability of a quilt. Choose wisely!

Basting

Basting takes time, but it is an important step that deserves your focus. If a quilt is securely basted, you will not have to worry about tucks or wobbly seams, and you will have the luxury of being able to start quilting anywhere on the quilt.

PIN BASTING

Pin basting is a simple method and much has already been written about it. I usually choose other methods as I find them more secure. Many top quilters pin baste, but I find that a pin will hold the fabric securely until I release it. A tuck that is forming at that point will then release into a new area, gathering even more volume, increasing the possibility of a tuck. This is more of a concern with high-loft batting, such as wool, or with fussy fabrics, such as silk.

SPRAY BASTING

Spray basting, properly done, will hold for well over a year. It is a secure hold and because of that it is a preferred method for many quilters. Spray basting with the quilt pinned to the wall makes it easier to remove tucks and align seams and is easier on the knees than spray basting on the floor. Always test fabric with the spray before committing. Some fabrics, such as silk, may stain.

It is a simple process. Begin by pinning the backing to the wall, wrong side facing out, with surrounding surfaces protected by newspapers. Smooth out the backing and spray evenly and lightly.

Pin the batting over the backing at the top and take care to smooth the batting to the backing, working half of the quilt at a time. Similarly, lightly spray the back of the quilt top and pin it to the wall to hold it while smoothing the top over the batting. Make sure all is well aligned. Again, work half of the quilt at a time.

You can baste large bed quilts on your own using this method and never have to get on your hands and knees!

COMBINED PIN AND MACHINE BASTING

My preferred method combines pin basting with machine basting. The added step is worth it: The end result is a rock-solid baste that will eliminate tucks.

Begin by pin basting as usual, placing pins in a grid, about a fist's width apart. Take the pin-basted quilt to the machine, which is threaded with water-soluble thread in the top and bobbin. Use a walking foot to stitch a line between the pins, using a 4.0 stitch length and loosened machine tension.

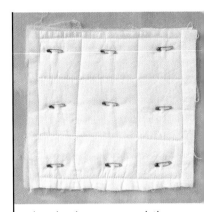

When the pins are removed, there is a secure grid of stitching to assure that there will be no tucks.

Remove the pins. Now you can quilt across that quilt top with nothing in your way!

MISTYFUSE BASTING

I use Mistyfuse (by Attached Inc.) to baste many of my quilts. Mistyfuse is a two-sided fusible with no paper backing or additives, just glue. It does not alter the hand of the fabric, yet securely fuses the quilt sandwich together, with no impediments to free-motion quilting.

For this method, place Mistyfuse on the wrong side of the backing of the quilt and place a Teflon fusing sheet atop. Fuse with a dry iron by lightly pressing. Let cool and peel off the sheet. Continue until the backing is fully fused.

For the quilt's front, tear pieces of Mistyfuse about 1″ square and place them about a fist's width apart across the wrong side of the front. Be sure to place some squares close to all of the edges. Fuse using a Teflon sheet.

On the ironing board, center the backing right side up atop the batting. Begin pressing in the center of the quilt and work outward, being careful to not create tucks. Do not press heavily with the iron; use a gentle touch.

Place the top face up on the fused batting and backing, center, and begin pressing lightly. Again work from the center out. Be mindful to not press hard with the iron and accidentally fuse the backing to the front through the batting. If the iron does not glide smoothly due to the texture of the fabric or piecing, lay a pressing cloth over the quilt and press through it.

Now you have a quilt securely basted with nothing on the quilt's surface to hinder your quilting!

Marking

Marking the lines to be quilted is something I do only if necessary. Many times I find that my marking has either disappeared before I can quilt or is hard to remove. But there are times—when quilting feathers or grids or when using stencils—when marking is needed. There are a wide variety of markers available including chalk, disappearing chalk, pencils, water-soluble markers, heat-erasable pens, and ceramic markers.

The most important considerations are that the mark be clear and crisp, that it stay visible through the quilting process, and that it be removed easily and completely once you have quilted the area.

There are many choices in marking tools. Try different types to see which works best for you.

The most reliable markers are water-soluble. They leave a clear line yet wash out easily. There are several types; blue washout markers or Crayola markers are the most commonly used.

Note that water-soluble marks can become permanent if the quilt comes into contact with heat. Heat can come from the iron, but it can also come from the sun (if the quilt is in a window or a parked car), a hot lamp, or even a sleeping cat. Also, if the quilt is washed with detergent before the marks are removed, the mark can set as a stain.

Any chalk or ceramic-based markers can be used on smaller projects, but they may wear off before quilting on larger projects. There are special pencils for use in quilt marking. Be sure to test on an inconspicuous spot of the quilt before committing to the whole piece. Some are very difficult to remove.

Heat-erasable pens have become popular with quilters for good reason. They leave a crisp line, the pen does not skip, they come in a wide array of colors, and they disappear with a puff of steam.

There are two issues with heat erasable pens, however. They sometimes leave a "ghost" mark after you steam the fabric, which will reappear in the cold. Test on your fabric first to see if the pen will leave a ghost mark. If the marks do reappear in the cold, toss the quilt in the dryer with a wet washcloth and the marks should go away again.

Tension and Stitch Length

Proper thread tension and stitch length is a beautiful thing—every stitch is well defined and the beauty of the thread shows.

If tension is off, one side of the quilting will have a line of thread and loops, without good definition of each stitch.

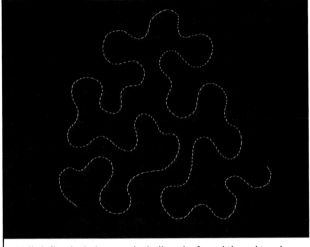

Well-defined stitches are the hallmark of good thread tension.

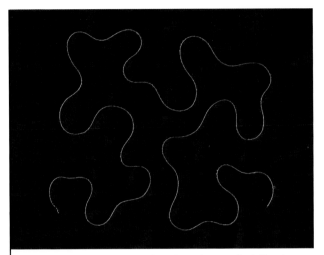

On one side of the quilt, the thread tension may look fine, but if the tension is off, the other side will have lines of thread with poorly defined stitches.

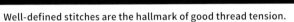

Good tension is worth pursuing. One of the easiest ways to think about tension is to imagine the top and bobbin threads as being in a tug-of-war. Good tension means that no one is winning, the sides are even.

Poor tension means one side is too tight and one too loose. Most tension issues can be addressed from the top thread tension, using the tension adjustment screen or dial on your machine.

DIAGNOSING AND FIXING TENSION

Poor tension can be easily diagnosed. Raise the presser foot and examine the stitches.

- If the bobbin thread shows on the top of the quilt, the top tension is too strong, pulling the bobbin thread to the top. Go to the top tension screen or dial and move it down in number.

- Conversely, if the top thread is showing on the back of the quilt, then the top tension is too loose. Go to the top tension screen or dial and increase the tension.

- When adjusting tension, make adjustments in small increments, ¼–½ number at a time. Stitch out a practice line in the seam or on a practice sandwich to determine whether the adjustment was adequate to achieve good tension.

TENSION TAKES TIME

Don't be surprised at how long it can take to get good tension. With a particularly challenging tension problem, I worked for several hours to get it just right! Be patient.

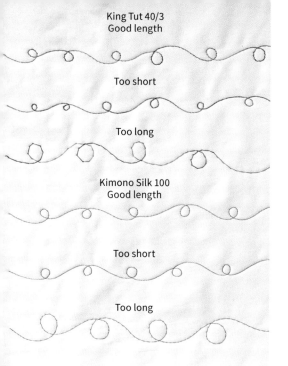

King Tut 40/3
Good length

Too short

Too long

Kimono Silk 100
Good length

Too short

Too long

The thicker thread (*upper*) looks best with a longer stitch length. The finer thread (*lower*) can have a smaller stitch length.

STITCH LENGTH

Proper stitch length also contributes to the beauty of the quilting. Remember, you are free-motion quilting, so the stitch length setting on the machine is irrelevant. You control stitch length with the speed of your hands and the machine.

Good stitch length shows the beauty of the thread. If the stitches are too long, the thread is floppy. Conversely, if the stitches are too short, the stitches stack up and mask the thread's beauty.

I've created a sample (at left) to show the effect of thread weight and stitch length on the beauty of the stitching. I've used two threads: a thicker 40-weight, three-ply cotton (King Tut by Superior Threads) on the top three rows and ultra-thin 100-weight silk (Kimono by Superior Threads) on the bottom three rows.

You will notice that the best stitch length will vary with the thickness of the thread. Thin threads can carry a smaller stitch length, while heavier threads require a longer stitch.

Take the time to adjust the tension and find the best stitch length for your thread so it will show beautifully on the surface of the quilt!

Hand Position

Your hands aren't just fabric movers, they are your stitch length regulator and provide the tension needed to help the quilt lie flat. Opinions vary, but I cringe when I see a quilter gripping the quilt with a clawed hand. Any gripping position can be hard on the hands if maintained for hours as you quilt, and it can stretch the quilt.

My preferred position, and the one I see most quilters use, is to "pet" the fabric, keeping the quilt taut between my gently outstretched hands. My hands are held with the thumbs inward, creating an inward-facing *L* with each hand. The area between the hands is about the size of a hot pad.

Avoid tenting the wrists up; keep the hand and forearm flat, resting gently upon the quilt. This seems to be the easiest position for most quilters.

Quilt the area within the "hot pad" of your hands. Once that area is quilted, stop, readjust the quilt, then move your hands to the new area. Do not move your hands to a new position with the machine running because you lose control of the stitching.

If you feel uncomfortable moving the quilt with the hand position I've described, experiment until you find a position that is comfortable for you. I recommend you avoid any approach that involves a closed-hand grip, however.

Photo by Jenny K. Lyon

Relax your hands on the surface of the quilt, surrounding the needle in an *L* shape.

WHOLE BODY EXPERIENCE

Free-motion quilting is a whole body experience, from your head to your toes! I want you to be aware of your entire body through comfortable ergonomics and a mindset of thoughtfulness and joy.

Quilting is more than a tactile and visual experience; it's also about the sound. I am mindful of the sound of my machine. I know the second my needle goes dull because I hear that *thump, thump*. I know when something has gone awry underneath my quilt because I hear it. I hear the sound of an empty bobbin. If you approach quilting this way, you will enjoy it even more!

Controlling Bulk

It can be difficult to handle a large quilt on a regular home sewing machine. I have successfully quilted queen-size quilts on my home machine and many have quilted king-size quilts on a domestic machine. It can be done.

Controlling the bulk of the quilt is key. Start with the most compact batting choice, as discussed in Batting (page 24).

If possible, place the machine's cabinet in a corner so the quilt cannot fall off the side or back of the table. And for ideas for strategically placing tables to control the quilt, see Surround (page 19).

Also consider how you handle the quilt as you quilt it. I "wear" my quilt as I am quilting it. I rest the quilt in my lap and gently place it around my shoulders. That lifts the weight of the quilt and allows it to move more smoothly. As I finish a section, I grab the quilt in my lap and pull up. That allows the quilt to feed smoothly into the machine.

Another option is to purchase a quilt suspension system. There are several choices available, and they all do the same thing: They lift the weight of the quilt off of the quilting table. The quilt moves easily and smoothly because almost all of the weight of the quilt is relieved. They are simple to use and make quilting so much easier and more pleasant!

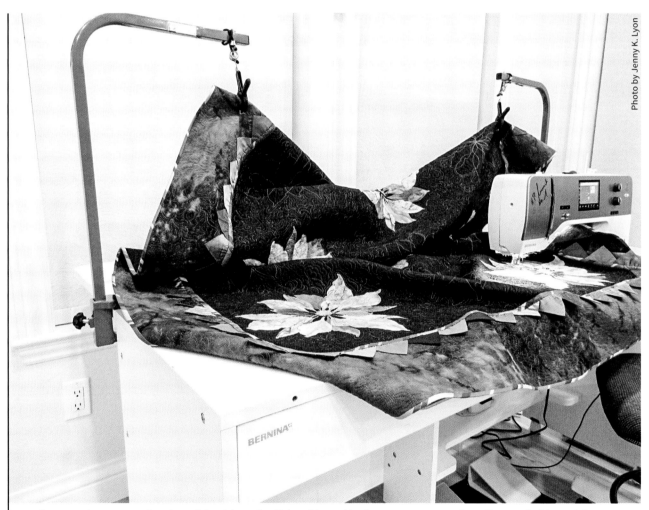

Photo by Jenny K. Lyon

A quilt suspension system takes the weight of the quilt off the table, making it very easy to move the quilt around. This one is by Patsy Thompson Designs.

STEP 1: 21 Days of "Plactice"

Now that you've made the best decisions for your machine-quilting setup, how do you go from a struggling free-motion quilter to a joyful and successful free-motion quilter?

> At the heart of my three-step program for free-motion quilting success is 21 days of play/practice. For simplicity, let's call it "**plactice**."

The program is simple: For 21 days, spend twenty minutes free-motion quilting on a quilt sandwich or small project. The object is to improve your skills a little bit at a time, without pressure for perfection.

Many of my students report that after 21 days of plactice, they feel confident enough to move onto more challenging projects. They have settled in and are *relaxed*, *excited*, and *confident* about free-motion quilting!

COMMITTING TO 21 DAYS OF "PLACTICE"

The commitment to plactice for 21 days is deceptively powerful. It sets a habit into motion and develops a strong skill set from small bits of time. Once you see yourself getting better, you'll be excited about quilting and your progress will be swift. It's a win-win!

Mindset

Let these 21 days of free-motion plactice be mindful yet playful. Relax into the process—it's only twenty minutes! Experiment with different motifs and types of free-motion quilting. Discover what you enjoy and what challenges you.

Try to set aside the time to plactice when you will be able to give it your best focus. For some, that might be early in the morning. For others, evening is best. Many of my students find it's easier to keep to the commitment if they plactice at the same time every day, but that's not necessary.

The object of the exercise is to feel loose and relaxed and to play around with free-motion stitching without stress. The simple commitment to 21 days of plactice will itself guide you to better free-motion quilting.

A small quilt sandwich makes it easy and simple to plactice; simply fill up that sandwich with the motif or pattern you want to improve upon.

"PLACTICE" TIMING

Remember, plactice for twenty minutes a day, no more, no less. You don't want to burn yourself out!

Don't be discouraged if you don't see results right away. My students frequently say their most significant progress happened toward the end of the 21 days. Just keep at it.

The 21-day period is not about achieving perfect—or even nearly perfect—quilting. It's about getting over the hump mentally and creating your own groove to settle into. You'll be amazed at how this habit sticks with you. It's like learning to ride a bike or drive a car—once you learn it, it will come back to you, even after a hiatus.

The Myth of Perfection

Students sometimes assume my work is nearly perfect. That is not the case! It has been said that perfection is the opposite of creativity. I enjoy seeing the "hand of the maker" on my quilts.

Perfection does not have a place in free-motion quilting in my opinion. When piecing, perfection in the ¼″ seam *is* important. In free-motion quilting, perfection is *not* important—the overall look of the quilt is. Very few viewers will notice uneven stitches or occasional glitches.

Free-motion quilting allows you to have the final say on how the quilt will look. It is more about the look you want than it is about perfect stitches.

"PLACTICE" HABITS

Try to keep your plactice as concentrated as possible, but don't worry if you skip a day or two, as long as you achieve 21 days of practice (page 30). Life sometimes interferes with our quilting intentions. Most days have twenty minutes to save for quilting.

THE SIX-FOOT RULE

Take time to step back and view your quilt as you go. View it in the manner in which it will ultimately be seen: For a bed quilt, view it on a bed; for a hanging, view it on a wall. Remember, most people will be viewing your work from a distance of at least 6 feet.

That bobble that seems horrific as you are quilting it may disappear when you get 6 feet away. Remember, when you are quilting, you have an abundance of light, you're 18″ away, and, if you're like me, you have assisted vision. No wonder that glitch looks awful to you.

Be kind to yourself and view your work-in-process from 6 feet away.

"Plactice" Sandwiches

Make quilt sandwiches before you start your 21 days. Then all you need to do is quilt for twenty minutes.

It might sound counterintuitive, but working on plactice squares can be liberating and enjoyable. Because it is not an actual project, there is no angst about the outcome—you can let loose and play!

The steps that follow will result in 24 quilt sandwiches. You may find you need more plactice sandwiches as you go, so this is a good "recipe" to follow.

Materials

100% cotton fabric: Good quality; either 6⅜ yards in a solid or near-solid color (so you can easily see your stitches) *or* 3¼ yards of 2 fabrics

Twin-size batting: Good quality; either 100% cotton *or* 80% cotton / 20% polyester

Thread: Good quality; one that will easily show on your fabric (Experiment with different types.)

1. Cut the fabric into squares approximately 14″ × 14″. You should get 48 squares.

2. Cut the batting into 14″ × 14″ squares.

3. Create 24 quilt sandwiches, placing a batting square between 2 fabric squares. You can hold the sandwiches

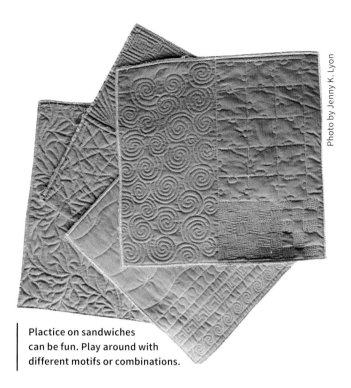

Plactice on sandwiches can be fun. Play around with different motifs or combinations.

together with five 1″ safety pins, but usually the batting is "grabby" enough to hold the layers on its own.

4. Prepare your sewing machine for free-motion quilting. Lower the feed dogs, put the machine in free-motion mode, insert a fresh needle, place the Teflon slider on the machine's bed, and choose the best free-motion foot for the machine.

The 21-Day Plan

It's playtime! Find twenty minutes in a day to simply sit at your machine and plactice. Don't make this complicated; just have fun. I have created a template to guide you through your 21 days. Consider this a suggestion and feel free to deviate if you want to plactice another way.

Here are a few tips before you get started.

- Keep a pencil and unlined paper at hand. Doodle on paper to figure out the path of new-to-you motifs. Don't erase if you don't get the motif; just start over on another part of the paper. Keep doodling until you figure out the path, and then move to fabric.

- Start at the bottom of an area and quilt upward. This may seem counterintuitive to you, but there is a reason: You can't see through the head of the machine. If you quilt from the top down, it's difficult to see behind the needle and make sure you don't run over an already quilted area. If you quilt from the bottom up, there are no worries about what's behind the machine, as it is unquilted.

- Remain mindful but relaxed as you plactice. Try not to hunch your shoulders up; keep your posture upright.

I'm not a great drawer. But doodles are about finding the quilting path, not about well-drawn motifs. Doodling connects the mind and the hands, readying you to free-motion quilt that motif.

Week 1: Build a Motif Inventory

The purpose of week one is to build up an inventory of versatile motifs. The more you have, the more fun you'll have, and the more personal your quilts will be.

Plactice (page 30) different types of motifs: borders, allover fills, grid or squiggly-line based motifs. You'll want a great variety of motifs for your real quilts, and you never know when a motif will come in handy. If you need some motif ideas, see Appendix of Quilting Motifs (page 92). Be open-minded—plactice them enough to conquer them.

STITCH A QUILT SANDWICH

Let's take the Snail Trail quilting motif (page 93) as an example.

1. Before stitching, mark the date on the quilt sandwich; this will help you track your progress. Take notes on the quilt sandwich about tips you want to remember or variations you want to try. Some quilters like to take daily notes in a sketchbook or create a portfolio of photos of daily progress. *Fig. A*

2. Starting at the bottom of a sandwich, leave about two-fingers width (or at least 1½˝) around the perimeter to allow room for your hands to rest on the quilt and maneuver it. This is important because you can't get good quilting right to the edge of a quilt; there needs to be room for your hand. *Fig. B*

TIMING

Set your phone or a timer for twenty minutes so that you don't have to keep checking. It makes for a more relaxed quilting session.

3. Quilt the Snail Trail design across the surface of the sandwich. Be mindful of your pace and find your niche speed. Relax as you quilt and note what parts are quilted best and why. Be observant of your pace and how the machine sounds. If you quickly conquered a motif on a particular day, try another motif until the twenty minutes is up. *Figs. C & D*

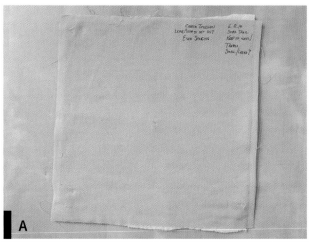

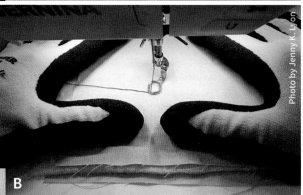

Photo by Jenny K. Lyon

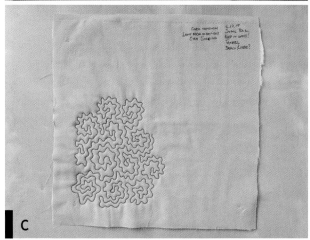

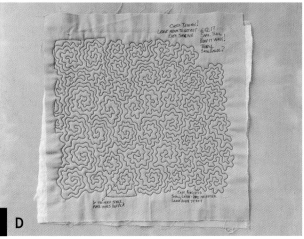

4. Each day choose another motif, either from the choices here or from other sources. Choose motifs and styles that you enjoy and you could imagine quilted on your quilts. The main thing is to keep going and find what you enjoy. *Figs. E–G*

You will see your progress build day by day. By the end of Day 7 you will have added several useful motifs to your usable inventory—congratulations!

DIFFICULT MOTIFS

If you find a particular motif difficult, try the process I call The Five-Square Rule.

1. Practice the motif first on paper until you "get it." If you're still having problems, try to describe out loud what you think you need to do. It will help you resolve the problem.

2. Once you have conquered the path on paper, go to the quilt sandwich. Mindfully fill up five 14″ × 14″ quilt sandwiches with the motif. After that, you're probably ready to put that on a quilt—it's just a matter of plactice.

LISTEN!

I need something to listen to while free-motion quilting. It helps me relax and get into the quilting zone. I might listen to a podcast, music, or even an undemanding TV program. I avoid anything intellectual because it requires too much concentration.

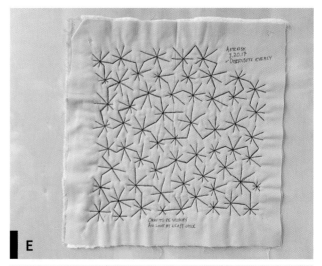

E

F

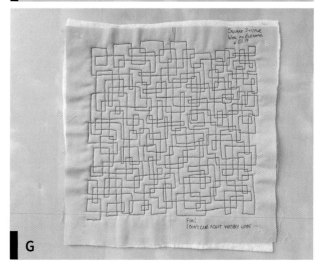

G

Week 2: Combine, Create, Find

This week is an opportunity to expand your choices by combining motifs that are already in your inventory, creating new motifs from what surrounds you, and finding new motifs from the work of others.

Each day this week choose to either combine, create, or find new motifs to plactice (page 30).

COMBINE MOTIFS

Combining motifs adds interest to quilting, and it's an easy way to create more quilting stories. Take a little time to sketch and play with the motifs you are already comfortable with.

One suggestion to get you started is a combination I call Flutter (page 93). Flutter combines a simple repeated S-curve with Half-Moons (page 92) and/or feathers. It is an elegant fill that can be a subtle background or a feature, depending on the thread choice and scale. A thin thread that matches the fabric would be subtle while a bold thread that contrasts would be a strong statement.

I recommend breaking Flutter down into its parts and quilting each before combining. As always, I recommend sketching this first before you start stitching.

1. Plactice the S-curve motif, echoing each one 2 or 3 times. On my sample I echoed each curve 3 times. Try to create space in between the curves for the Half-Moons or feathers. Think of those empty spaces as vessels to hold feathers and Half-Moons. You might want to trace my path with your finger to get the gist of how I quilted this sample. *Fig. H*

2. On paper, plactice the Half-Moons and feathers, roughly approximating the spaces created in Step 1. Draw those spaces out on the plactice sandwich and fill them with feathers or Half-Moons. If you're not quilting great feathers, use the Half-Moons motif instead. *Fig. I*

3. Combine the curves, feathers and/or Half-Moons on paper before you quilt and consider tracing the path I took on my sample. Once you have some confidence, move to the plactice sandwich. *Fig. J*

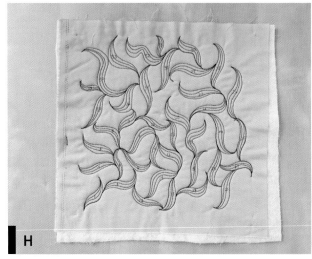

H

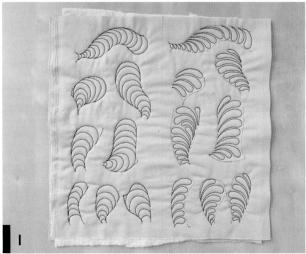

I

J

If you reach a point where you are not sure what to do next, stop and trace a possible path with your finger. This will help you resolve the decision. Don't expect your first try to be perfect; have fun with it and learn from any mistakes you make.

Sketch an inventory of the motifs you know and experiment with combinations. Once you figure out the path on paper, it will be easy to stitch, and you'll be creating your own combinations.

Daisies (page 92) and Bubbles (page 92) is another of my favorite combinations. The steps for this combination are included in the Boho Cutout Denim Jacket project (page 62).

Combine motifs to create an elegant flow for a background without detracting from the focus. In this case, I chose to use a thin thread that matched the background, creating a subtle statement—exactly what I wanted in *Morning Breeze* (page 80).

One fun way to plactice is to quilt your name and surround it with motifs. This is a great way to experiment with combining motifs before you commit to them on a quilt.

CREATE MOTIFS

As I discussed in Inspiration (page 7), you are surrounded by design: logos, commercial packaging, print ads, fabric from your stash, the decor in your home, and even upholstery fabrics and wallpaper. Use that inspiration to create new motifs to plactice.

FIND MOTIFS

With a simple web search under "free-motion fillers" or "free-motion motifs," you will find an abundance of free material rich with ideas. Take a few moments before your quilting session to find some fresh new ideas.

Here are some sites to try:

Pinterest (pinterest.com): Type "free-motion motifs" in the search bar.

Leah Day (leahday.com): Leah Day uses videos and drawings to show more than 365 quilting designs.

The Inbox Jaunt (theinboxjaunt.com): Lori Kennedy posts free-motion designs daily.

The Quilting Company (quiltingcompany.com): Click the Discover & Learn tab. This site covers a variety of quilting topics daily.

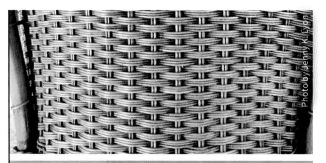

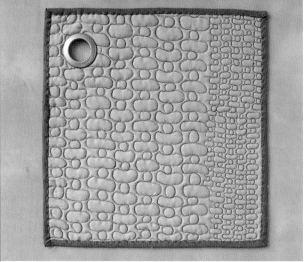

A wicker chair inspires a quilting motif.

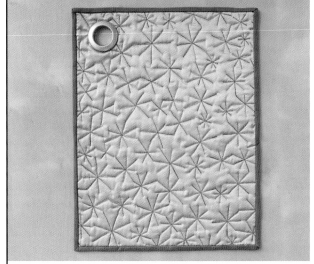

A succulent bloom inspires an Asterisk (page 92) motif.

Week 3: Quilt Small Items

It's time to put that glorious plactice (page 30) onto something that can be used and shared! You may not be ready to jump into a full project, so here are a few suggestions for micro projects that can be completed in a weekend.

ONWARD

"Onward" is my mantra, my guidepost. I have muddled my way through quilting. At first I did anything that struck my fancy, and I was okay with that. I knew I had to explore to find my niche. I made a few bed quilts and tried various techniques and styles. Ultimately I settled into primarily wholecloth art quilts. But that could change!

As I stumbled through the years, I frequently found myself ripping out work that was not perfect. Then I had an epiphany. While working on a garment ensemble, I became unhappy with my feathers on part of the jacket. So I ripped that section out. My new stitching was so much better.

After I finished that section, I realized that now, my new stitching was better than what I left in. If I ripped that out, then the newest stitching would be better than what I just did!

That is when I adopted the mantra of "Onward." I decided that unless the entire trajectory of what I was doing was unacceptable, I would finish up that project and fix the "bad" decisions on the *next* project.

That has been my guiding principle ever since: Onward. I'll fix that problem on the next quilt! I hope you adapt a similar attitude of grace and forgiveness for yourself. You *will* produce some less-than-exceptional work; you *will* make things that you don't love. That's okay. Don't stop. Onward!

PLACE MATS

Place mats are a great project on which to plactice multiple motifs. The focus here is on quilting, so this project calls for a front and back of yardage, not pieced tops. Of course, you are welcome to piece if you'd like.

These place mats will be reversible; you can get two looks by choosing different but complementary fabrics. Think about whether you want the quilting to show when choosing fabrics. A busy print will hide less-than-lovely quilting.

Four place mats require a total of 2 yards of fabric, or 1 yard of 2 fabrics, and ½ yard for binding. Cut a total of 8 pieces 18″ × 16″. The finished place mats will be 16″ × 14″, so the extra 2″ gives a little space for your hands to rest as you quilt. Cut 4 pieces of batting 18″ × 16″.

Baste the 3 layers together using your favored method, making sure the edges are aligned.

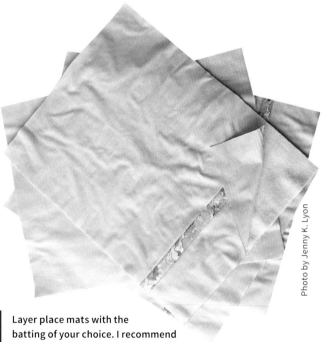

Photo by Jenny K. Lyon

Layer place mats with the batting of your choice. I recommend cotton since place mats will be washed frequently.

Various Wavy Lines with Motifs (page 94), Bubbles (page 92), and Daisies (page 92) motifs

A Stipple (page 92) variation with straight lines and Peacock (page 93) motifs

Alternate Grid (page 94) with Bubbles (page 92), Stipple (page 92) variation with straight lines, and Branch (page 93) variation to make leaves variation motifs

Orange Peel (page 94) and Feathers (page 94) motifs

Quilt rows of a variety of motifs, combine motifs, or quilt an allover design. This is a chance to play with what you've accomplished over the last two weeks.

Trim each place mat to 16″ × 14″. Bind as you would a quilt. Cut a 2¼″ binding, fold in half, and then stitch to the place mat edge using a ¼″ seam. Join the ends, flip the binding over, and hand stitch to the back of the place mat.

FOUND QUILT BLOCKS

I always keep an inventory of found blocks around—they are excellent plactice (page 30) pieces! You may have some extra quilt blocks lying around that currently have no intended purpose. Or you may find orphaned blocks at garage sales or thrift shops. One great source of quilt blocks is quilt guild shows; there is usually a garage-sale type area where you can purchase abandoned quilt squares.

Layer them individually and experiment with a new quilting plan. I have also assembled them together and treated them as a quilt; even if I don't intend to finish it, the pieced top is great to plactice or audition upon.

Stars 'n' Stripes, 46″ × 46″, 2012

My *Stars 'n' Stripes* quilt was made from unused orphan blocks that I had lying around. I love quilting feathers and wanted to quilt something that allowed me to fill the surface with feathers. Happily, *Stars 'n' Stripes* became that quilt.

Found quilt squares are great for placticing—you didn't have to construct them!

Hot pads made with found blocks

AUDITIONING A NEW MOTIF

To audition a new motif or style, quilt in the normal fashion except make the top tension very loose. After you have viewed the completed quilting, turn it over and pull the bobbin thread out. It will come out very easily, and you will be able to audition yet another motif or style on that same piece.

CHARITY QUILT

A charity quilt can be a part of your twenty minutes of plactice. I typically quilt a charity quilt with a playful allover motif, which makes it especially easy to quilt in twenty-minute segments.

Most quilt guilds have a charity quilt program with kits to make the quilt. Because they are smaller quilts, they quilt up quickly yet provide a good-size space to plactice on. If you're concerned about your less-than-perfect quilting (and I hope you're not!), opt for busy prints to hide your stitches.

If you choose an allover motif and a large scale, a cuddle-size charity quilt can be completed in a few hours. The recipient will be thrilled to receive your gift, and you will have contributed back to your own community.

GIVE JOY

Please don't be critical of your quilting on a charity quilt! Imagine if you were experiencing a difficult time and someone gave you a less-than-perfectly quilted quilt. Would you be upset? Wouldn't you instead just love the fact that someone made a quilt to comfort you? I would, and I'll bet you would too! Give joy to someone else by making a charity quilt, no matter how it's quilted.

Photo by Jenny K. Lyon

Charity quilts are perfect places to plactice. They are "real" quilts but there should be no stress over less-than-perfect quilting.

Looking Back

Your 21-day journey is now complete. I know your confidence and skills have significantly improved. Look back at where you started and compare that quilting to your Week 3 quilting—what a difference! You have not only improved your quilting but you now have a wider variety of motifs, fills, borders, combinations, and allover designs to choose from.

With all those choices and combinations available to you, it's going to be even more fun to quilt. Your quilts will become more personal as the breadth of your quilting motif inventory increases. Your personal style will become something to treasure. Are you ready to move on to some projects?

STEP 2: Five to Learn On

These projects are suggestions to get you placticing (page 30) on projects that are approachable and fun and will build skills and confidence. It's the next step and will prepare you to begin quilting your own larger and more challenging projects.

The time needed to complete these projects runs from a few hours for a postcard to a few days for a quilt-from-the back quilt or quilt-as-you-go quilt. And each one is a delight to stitch!

Fabric Postcards

The small format of a postcard is a great place to try new free-motion quilting ideas. With minimal investment in time and materials, you can share your creativity with friends and family. Wouldn't you be touched if a friend sent *you* a fabric postcard?

Petunia, 4″ × 6″

Fabric postcards can be sent in the mail with a regular stamp as long as they meet basic criteria: They must be 4″ × 6″ and no thicker than ⅛″. They can be embellished with small beads and flat sequins that are securely fastened and will not get damaged in the mailing process. If a postcard is not within those standards, you can still send it by putting it into an envelope with appropriate postage.

You may want to try a variety of techniques on postcards. The ones here feature free-motion quilting, but you can use machine or hand embroidery, collage, photo transfer, and so much more.

All cards will have a decorative top, structural middle, and an address side, with some sort of fusing required to hold all three layers together.

POSTCARD BOOK

An excellent source of information on more fabric postcard techniques can be found in Franki Kohler's *Fast, Fun & Easy Fabric Postcards* (by C&T Publishing).

Materials

Heavy interfacing: 5″ × 7″ piece (such as fast2fuse HEAVY Interfacing, Timtex, or other sturdy two-sided fusible) or use batting (See Using Batting, page 24.)

Decorative fabrics: For front of postcard; use fabrics such as quilting or decorator fabric, sheer or shiny fabric, garment fabric, or fragments of old textiles like hankies or baby blankets

Solid or near solid fabric: 5″ × 7″ piece for back (address) side of postcard (I prefer a thicker woven solid, such as Kona cotton in nonwhite, to avoid show-through.)

Two-sided fusible (optional)

Teflon pressing sheet

Top thread: Do *not* use nylon, as it may melt during the fusing process.

Bobbin thread: I recommend a thin, white thread to keep it from shadowing through the backing.

Rotary cutter and mat

Quilter's ruler: At least 6″ × 12″

Viewfinder (optional): 4″ × 6″ piece of sturdy card stock

USING BATTING

Note that if you use batting, the postcard may need to be sent in an envelope due to its thickness. Also, fuse together each batting layer for stability.

FAST2FUSE

My preferred postcard material is fast2fuse HEAVY Interfacing (by C&T Publishing) because it is sturdy but not too thick, and its adhesive is excellent. If you can find fast2fuse on the bolt, buy the cut in multiples of 7″. You will be cutting it into pieces 5″ × 7″, so one 7″ × 20″ strip (the bolt is 20″ wide) will yield 4 postcards.

Make the Postcard

1. Place the base fabric for the front of the postcard on the surface wrong side up and place the interfacing or batting over it. *Fig. A*

2. Flip the postcard over and loosely assemble the fabrics and/or embellishments on the base fabric. Don't worry about the fabrics falling beyond the edge of the postcard for now. If you are attaching more than one layer of fabric, apply a two-sided fusible to the back of the top fabric and attach to the postcard. If you're not sure of the placement, tack each one into place with a quick touch with the tip of a hot iron; they can easily be removed and repositioned. *Fig. B*

3. Use the viewfinder, if desired, to see how your design fits in the postcard size. Note that the outside ⅝″ perimeter of fabric will be either cut off or used for edge treatment. *Fig. C*

4. Once you are confident of the fabric placements, fuse the fabric to the postcard center according to manufacturer's instructions. Place the Teflon sheet on an ironing board to protect it from the fusible on the back. *Fig. D*

5. Cut off excess fabrics around the edge of the postcard using a rotary cutter and ruler, but keep the size at about 5″ × 7″. *Fig. E*

6. Add any free-motion quilting now before embellishments. Because there is only ½″ excess postcard material around the edges, it can be difficult to get a secure grip to free-motion quilt. Grip the 2 diagonal corners of the postcard with your fingers to make this easier. *Fig. F*

7. Add any other final embellishments, such as beading, couching, or embroidery, if desired. Fuse the back (address side) fabric to the postcard. *Fig. G*

8. Cut the postcard to 4″ × 6″. Secure the edges of the postcard. The easiest method and the one I use most often is a simple satin-stitched edge. Use a thicker thread and go around twice to completely cover the edges. You can get creative with the edge treatment and couch yarn or add a traditional binding instead. Variegated threads add a nice final touch to the edge. *Fig. H*

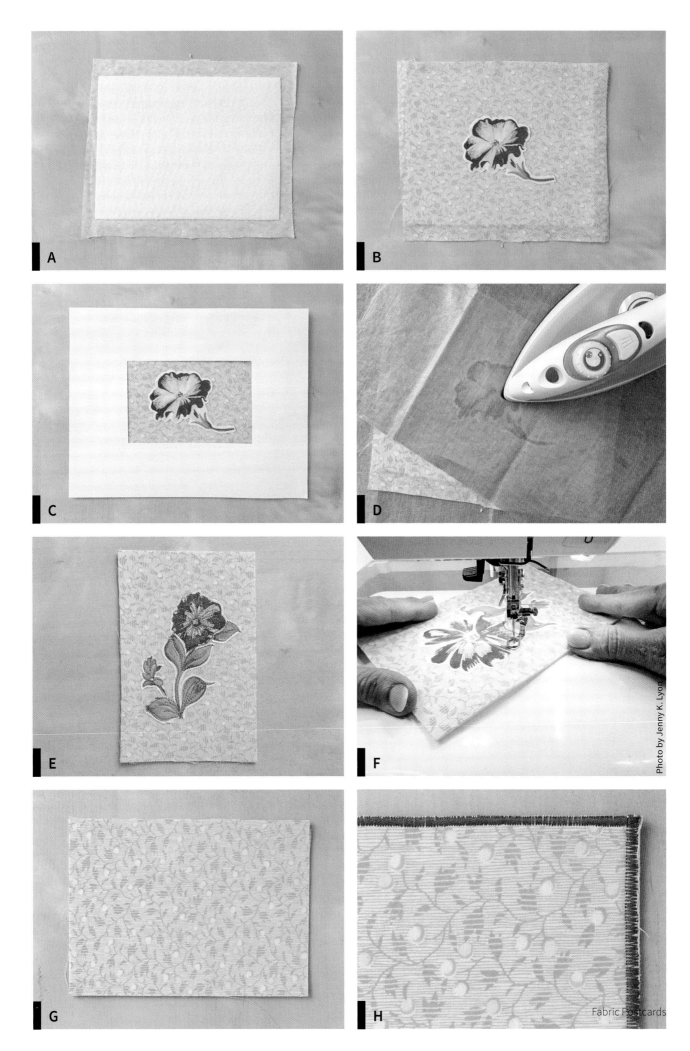

Postcard, 4″ × 6″, Barbara Hunter

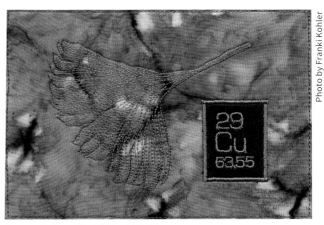

Copper Ginkgo, 4″ × 6″, Franki Kohler

White Sunflower, 4″ × 6″, Franki Kohler

Feathers, 4″ × 6″

Spring Chicks, 4″ × 6″

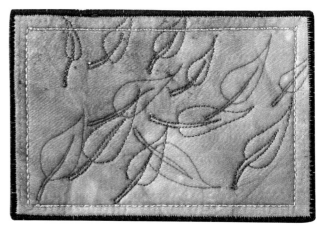

Falling, 4″ × 6″

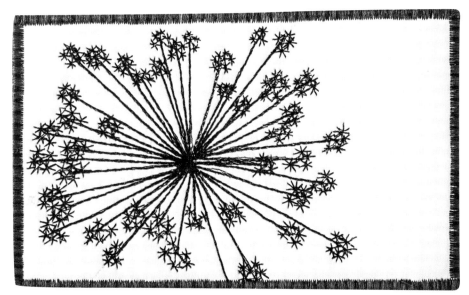

Queen Anne's Lace, 4″ × 6″

Butterflies, 4″ × 6″

Toile, 4″ × 6″

Panel Quilts

Preprinted panels are a great way to experiment with technique, batting, thread, and design choices as you improve your free-motion quilting skills. There are so many great panels available now that there is surely one that appeals to you. And if it does not turn out well, you have made a minimal investment in time and materials and learned what not to do!

Photo by Jenny K. Lyon

I chose the Thicket panel set by Moda. I liked the idea of four small panels (they each measure 17½″ × 22½″) that allowed me to experiment with four different concepts on a small scale—perfect!

Fox, 24″ × 28″

Materials

Preprinted panel

Batting: 1 piece, at least 5″–8″ larger than panel and borders on all sides

Backing: 1 piece, at least 5″–8″ larger than panel and borders on all sides

---

Make the Panel Quilt

1. Cut the panel to the desired size. *Fig. A*

2. Add borders to the panel as desired. I added an inset and a border that I mitered, as I also wanted to improve my mitered corners. Create a quilt sandwich with the batting and backing. Baste as desired. *Fig. B*

A

B

3. Mark the panel for quilting, if needed. I chose to keep the quilting simple by radiating lines from the center that would emphasize the fox. This did require marking. I folded to find the center of the panel and then placed tick marks every inch around the perimeter. I marked each line, extending it from the center to each tick mark. *Fig. C*

4. Complete the quilting. Trim and bind the panel to finish.

LEAVE ROOM FOR YOUR HANDS!

With anything that I quilt, I cut the backing and batting large enough to accommodate the width of my palm. This allows me to confidently quilt all the way up to the edge of the top.

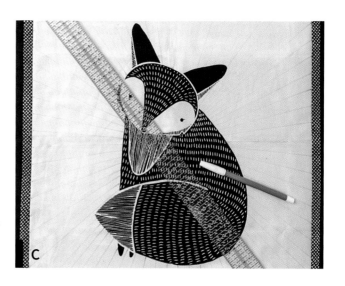

Bear, 22″ × 26″

Bear in process

> I thought the Bear panel was the most adorable of the bunch! I wanted to put a feminine flair on him. Once I added the filigree border, I knew it needed curves. I wanted to improve my morphing skills by playfully mixing multiple motifs over the background.

I did do some doodling first for the background morphing. I created an inventory of motifs I wanted to include: Daisies (page 92), Bubbles (page 92), and a Half-Moon variation to resemble feathers (page 94).

As I was quilting this panel, I frequently stopped and put it up on my design wall. As a result, I made several course-corrections along the way.

Rabbit, 25″ × 29″

The Rabbit panel challenged me, perhaps because I forgot to start out with a mission statement (page 13). As I was adding on the border, I spontaneously decided to add random tiny prairie points. I love the little spark they add! Bubbles (page 92) were the perfect fill for the center.

I was very excited about the border, which was based on a quilt by Margo Clabo. This ruler work was a little more challenging, but I really like the end result.

Owl, 23˝ × 27˝

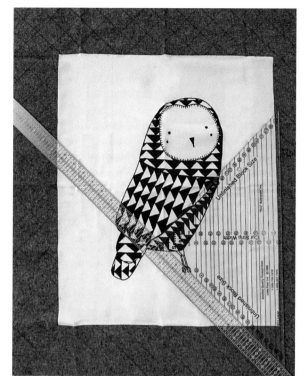

The border on *Owl* was challenging.

> The owl was my biggest challenge. I wanted to make him decidedly masculine, which is outside of my normal aesthetic. I started with a gridded border but then decided he would look even more masculine if it became a bit of a plaid, which involved a lot more marking than I anticipated.

I chose a very thick thread for the red "plaid," a decision that required over an hour of work in order to get good tension with my white bobbin thread.

For the masculine background, I doodled quite a bit to figure out the grid-based meandering. It was well worth my time. This is my husband's favorite of the bunch, so I must have achieved my goal of a masculine panel.

Quilt-from-the-Back Quilt

There's an easy way to achieve impressive quilting on the front of a quilt: Choose a printed fabric for the backing and quilt from the back! The process is straightforward. The quilt is assembled in the normal manner with the top, batting, and backing. But for quilting, put the back side of the quilt up, and quilt around the motifs in the print. When you flip the quilt over, the front will show beautiful and seemingly complex quilting!

Jane's Garden, 42″ × 60″, 2017

Quilting in this manner gives you an opportunity to hone your skills by following the lines already printed on the backing. If you don't always hit the line, it will not readily show. This method is an easy way to achieve an impressive finish. Choose the backing fabric carefully and you'll be pleased with the result. You'll be able to plactice on a whole quilt without stressing over the quilting path. Have fun!

My initial inspiration for this project was a Jane Sassaman large-scale print fabric. Although the scale is huge, the motif outlines are close together, creating a scale that is appropriate for this size of quilt. I took the colors from the backing as a cue for my fabric choices. The simply pieced front allows the quilting to shine.

Choose Fabric

The quilting is determined by your backing fabric choice.

Consider the following when choosing the backing fabric:

- Find a fabric you find interesting and fun to work with.

- Choose a fabric with motifs that are simple enough to stitch around. Complex fabrics with a lot of nooks and crannies in the design would be difficult to quilt. With your finger, try to trace a continuous quilting line. Is the design too complex for this?

- Look for a fabric with a scale that is appropriate for the style, size, and use of the quilt. A larger quilt would benefit from an especially large-scale print, whereas a baby quilt could take a more petite print. A motif as big as your hand would work beautifully on a bed quilt but may not work on a small project.

- Think about the end use of the quilt. A cuddling or child's quilt needs to be soft and would benefit from loose quilting. A decorative quilt could be quilted more densely.

- Create a test sample out of a fat quarter of fabric and quilt it. Make sure it is quilt-able and not too fussy.

- Keep in mind that almost all fabrics will need some fudging to get from one motif to another. You might need to Loops (page 92) or Stipple (page 92) from one motif to another.

These fabrics would work well as backing fabrics.

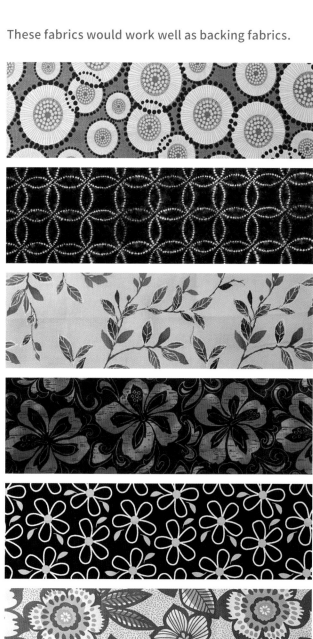

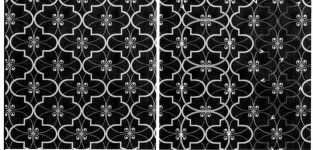

Note that this last fabric has two possible quilting patterns: one on the pink path and one on the green path.

Materials

Completed quilt top

Batting: 5″–8″ larger than quilt top

Backing: 5″–8″ larger than quilt top

Prepare to Quilt

1. Before you begin to layer and quilt, take a moment to make sure the materials work well together.

- If you want your quilting to be highlighted, consider a lofty batting. If your project is to be well used and washed frequently, a cotton or cotton blend would be a good choice.

- Thread requires similar thought: Heavier threads will stand up and be noticed on the top, thinner threads will sink it. It depends on the look you want and the intended use. For my project, I chose wool batting to highlight the quilting and a thicker thread (King Tut by Superior Threads) because I wanted the stitching to be prominent.

- Make sure the backing is an appropriate style and scale for the quilt top.

2. Make a photocopy of the backing fabric and practice moving your finger in a continuous line as though you were quilting. Become familiar with the path before you begin to quilt.

3. Create a small 14″–18″ plactice quilt sandwich of fabric similar to or the same as the quilt top with the same batting and backing as your quilt. Use this to test the tension, thread, and needle to avoid having to take out stitching from the quilt top.

Quilt

1. Layer the quilt and baste using your preferred method. *Fig. A*

2. If you have securely basted the quilt, you can start anywhere. Once you have quilted about 1 square foot, stop the stitching line and view the quilt from the front to make sure you are happy with the thread choice, tension, and quilting path.

When I first began quilting my sample quilt, I was quilting some of the more intricate parts of the motif. When I flipped it over and viewed the small area I had quilted, I realized that those details were not necessary. Fortunately I caught it early enough that I did not have to take out the over-quilted areas. *Fig. B*

3. Once you are happy with your choice, relax and enjoy the quilting. Don't stress if you are not hitting the lines of the motif exactly. You can't tell from the front of the quilt.

4. Trim and bind the quilt to finish. *Fig. C*

Some large-scale prints lend themselves to a wholecloth format. In this case, the quilting could stand alone as the front of a quilt without any piecing.

Quilt-as-You-Go Quilt

Quilt-as-you-go (QAYG) is an excellent method that allows large quilts to be easily quilted on a domestic machine. Most QAYG methods require a block setting and/or sashing as well as a lot of hand sewing.

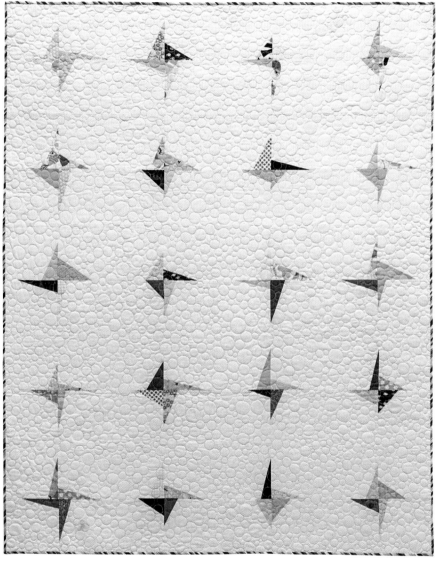

Summer Stars, 48˝ × 60˝

I prefer the cut batting method because it is not dependent upon a block-formatted quilt top and does not require any hand stitching. In this method, the batting is divided into halves, thirds, or quarters, and quilting begins with only one section of batting in the middle. After all, the batting is what causes the most bulk of a quilt.

Eliminating most of the batting makes it possible to quilt even a king-size quilt on a domestic machine! Once you try this method you will find it useful on any larger quilt whether the quilt top is medallion, block, or wholecloth. Your quilting will not only be easier but better because the entire quilt moves with ease by controlling the batting. Try it!

Materials

Completed quilt top

Batting: 5″–8″ larger than quilt top

Backing: 5″–8″ larger than quilt top

Prepare to Quilt

1. Starch and press the top and backing. Spray baste the back side of the top and backing. I find spray basting to be especially well suited for this method because it gives a very secure hold and it's easier to manipulate the cut batting and quilt top. I prefer to baste on the wall, protecting the surrounding surfaces with newspapers. This can also be done horizontally on a table or floor. *Fig. A*

2. Analyze the top and decide whether you want to split the batting in halves, thirds, or even quarters if it is a large quilt. You'll want the batting joins to be somewhere other than on a piecing line, and you'll want the pieces to be somewhat even in size. Also, if you are planning to quilt a motif larger than a few inches, you'll need to make sure that you can complete an entire motif without running off the batting. *Fig. B*

A

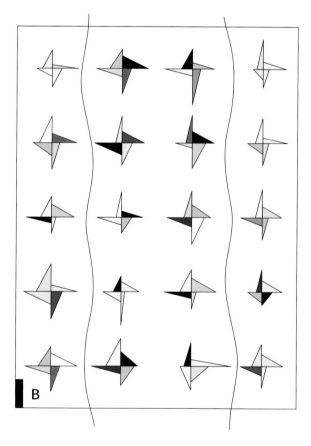

B

3. Cut the batting in sections to your determined sizes, cutting with a gentle wavy line using a rotary cutter. Avoid straight lines, as they are more likely to show through to the front of the quilt. *Fig. C*

4. Mark each section of batting at the bottom so the puzzle pieces of batting will go together nicely when you reassemble. I usually write *CL* on the left edge of the center piece, *CR* on the right edge of the center piece, *L* on the left side piece, and *R* on the right side piece. *Fig. D*

5. Find the center of the quilt top, the backing, and the center batting piece. Place a mark at this spot on the top and bottom edge of each. *Fig. E*

6. Place the center section of batting on the quilt backing, aligning centers. Be sure it lays straight and has no ridges or puckers. Pat it firmly to assure that it is securely adhered to the back. Add the quilt top, again aligning centers, making sure it is straight with no puckers or ridges. Pat firmly to adhere. *Fig. F (next page)*

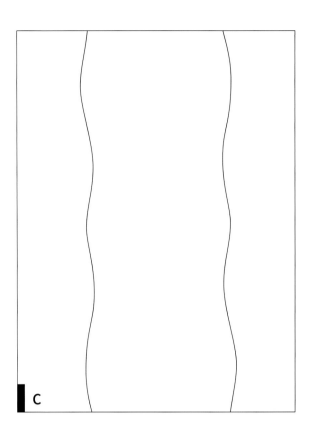

C

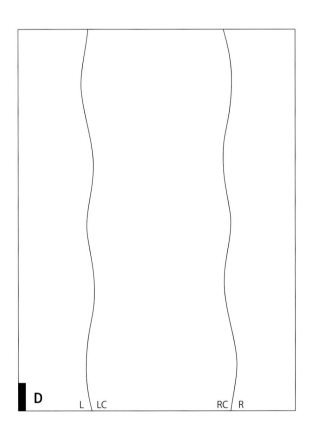

D   L   LC   RC   R

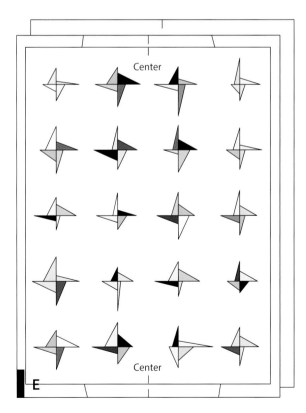

E

Quilt

1. Make sure you know where the batting ends, either by feel or visually by clues on the quilt top. You can also place pins close to the edge of the batting to know where it is. Quilt as you would any other quilt, checking to be sure you are not running off the batting. *Fig. F*

If the quilt is a block format or has regularly spaced motifs, plan your quilting so that you finish a motif within the section of batting. If you have motifs that do extend beyond the area of batting, stop the quilting at a point where it will be easy to reconnect with the next round of quilting.

2. Remove the quilt from the machine. Place on a horizontal surface and flip the quilt top back to the left to expose the right side of the backing. Align the edges of the right batting piece with the center batting piece; straighten, smooth, and pat firmly. There should be no gaping or overlapping of the batting. You may have to fuss with it a little bit to get everything well aligned. *Fig. G*

The spray baste should hold the batting join well, but if you want extra security, there are two options. You can use fusible batting tape to adhere the sections

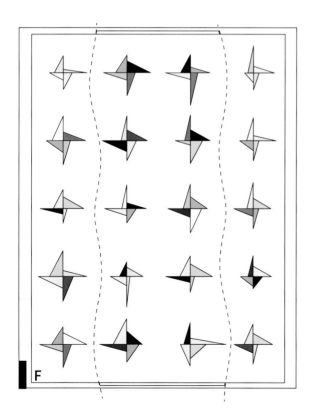

F

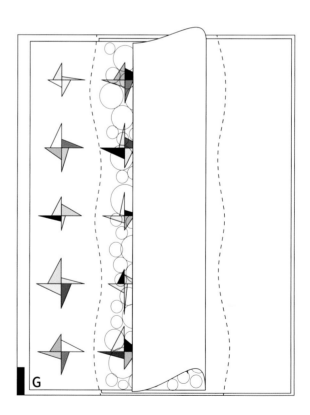

G

securely to each other, leaving no bulk. If you are careful, you can steam the tape onto the batting while it rests on a table or slide a flat ironing pad along the length as you go up the join. Alternatively, hand baste the two batting sides together with a thin thread that matches the color of the batting. Whatever method you choose, make sure that it does not show through to the front of the quilt.

3. Flip the quilt top back onto the right side. Smooth and straighten the quilt top over the batting. *Fig. H*

4. Quilt that section as usual, blending the quilting from one section to another. Stop and check that there is no visible line where one section stopped and the new one began. *Fig. I*

5. Add the last section in the same manner, blending and checking before completing the quilting. *Fig. J*

6. Trim and bind the quilt to finish.

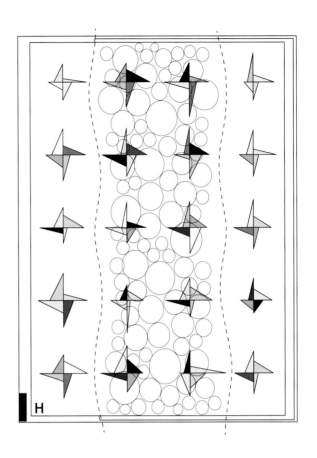

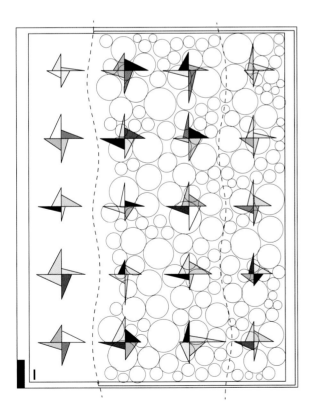

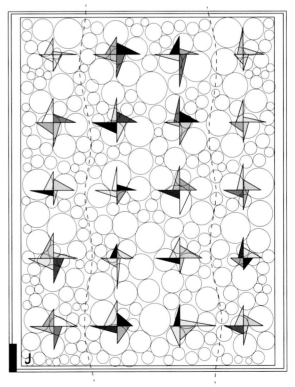

Boho Cutwork Denim Jacket

You can create this custom leather-look cutwork jacket in a weekend with minimal supplies and a purchased denim jacket. Each line is stitched twice—the first pass is about learning to freehand stitch motifs and the second pass is about trying to hit the previous line. And if you don't hit the line, it will not show, so enjoy the process of creating your jacket!

Materials

Purchased denim jacket: Use one with a center panel on back of jacket, in a style that fits and flatters your figure.

kraft-tex (by C&T Publishing): 1 roll in Natural color

KRAFT-TEX

Choose from three lines of kraft-tex to use in this jacket:

Basics: Unwashed. Comes in 5 colors (Natural, White, Black, Stone, Chocolate). *To use for this jacket, prewash it for a softer feel.*

Vintage: Prewashed. Comes in 5 colors (Natural, White, Black, Stone, Chocolate). *This already has the softer feel, so it's ready to sew!*

Designer: Prewashed. Hand-dyed. Comes in 6 colors (Blue Iris, Greenery, Marsala, Orchid, Tangerine, Turquoise). *To use for this jacket, prewash it—the hand-dyed colors may bleed slightly when washed.*

Medium-heavy quilting thread: I used 40/3 King Tut by Superior Threads.

Topstitch needle: In size appropriate for thread (probably 90/14)

Sharp, sturdy scissors: With blade no longer than 3½˝ (See Choosing the Right Scissors, below.)

Temporary marker: Such as blue washout marker or ceramic lead marker

Tracing paper: 11˝ × 17˝ piece

Hera Marker (by Clover)

Paper scissors

Walking foot (optional): Not required, but very useful

Packing paper (optional): To practice drawing the stitching line

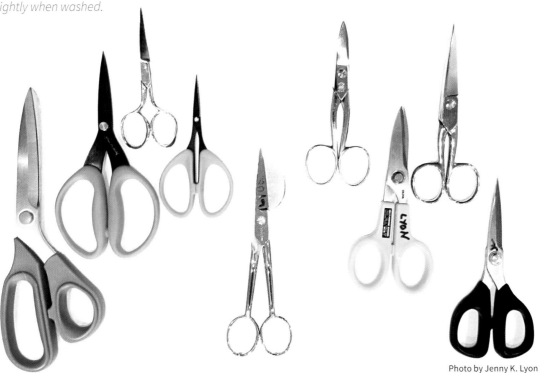

Photo by Jenny K. Lyon

CHOOSING THE RIGHT SCISSORS

The scissors on the right in this image are the best for cutwork because they have short sturdy blades. The scissors on the left are the least effective for cutwork. The blades on the dressmaker shears on the far left are too long, the blades on the next three are too thin, and the duckbill scissors would be difficult to use.

Prepare the Jacket

1. Determine the size of the back panel by laying the tracing paper down on the panel. Run your finger back and forth along the seams to create a line on the tracing paper that records the size of the panel. *Figs. A & B*

2. Use this as the pattern piece to cut out the kraft-tex. Use the Hera Marker to transfer the dimensions from the tracing paper onto the kraft-tex. Add approximately ¾″ all around the perimeter of the outline and cut with a pair of paper scissors. *Fig. C*

3. Place the kraft-tex over the wrong side of the center back panel of the jacket. Secure with several sturdy pins along the outside seamline. *Fig. D*

4. Flip the jacket right side up. Using the walking foot on the sewing machine and a medium-heavy quilting thread, stitch the kraft-tex to the jacket from the right side of the jacket.

First, stitch just inside the panel seam. Line up the sewing machine needle so that it is barely to the inside of the jacket's seamline. Your needle should rub up against the jacket's seam. *Fig. E*

Sew along all 4 sides of the center back panel using the walking foot. The kraft-tex will be on the underside of the stitching line. Overlap the ends of the stitching line by 8–10 stitches. This will secure the stitching line.

5. Create a second row of stitching to secure the kraft-tex by stitching over the inner row of topstitching on the jacket. Overlap the stitches again by 8–10 stitches. *Fig. F*

A

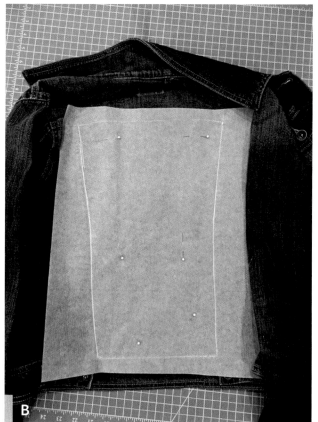

B

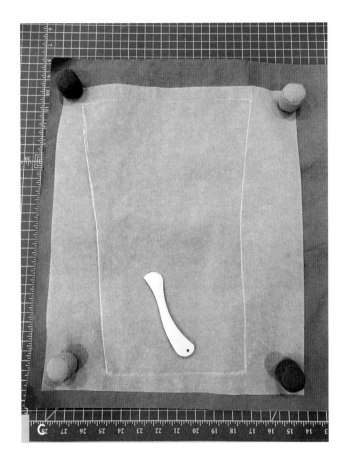

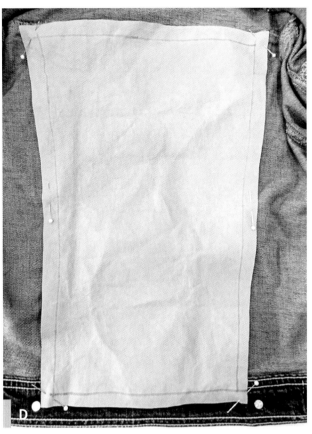

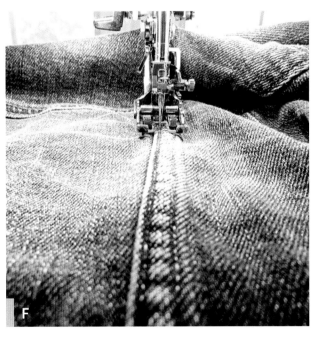

Photos on these facing pages by Jenny K. Lyon

6. Lightly mark the position of the Daisies (page 92) on the jacket with the temporary marker by randomly drawing circles about the size of your fist across the panel. Leave 1–3 finger widths between them. You might want to create a partial daisy as a design element. Mark the approximate center of each daisy. *Fig. G*

Prepare to Quilt

1. Before starting to quilt, take a small piece of kraft-tex and free-motion quilt it to the jacket to test the tension and make adjustments before starting. This piece will be easy to unpick once you get the tension right. *Fig. H*

2. Plactice drawing the Daisies (page 92) and Bubbles (page 92) with a continuous line on a piece of packing paper. The larger size of the paper will allow you to draw the size at which you will quilt it. *Figs. I–L*

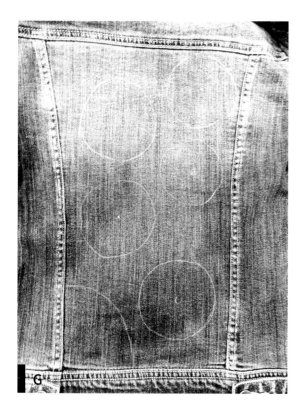

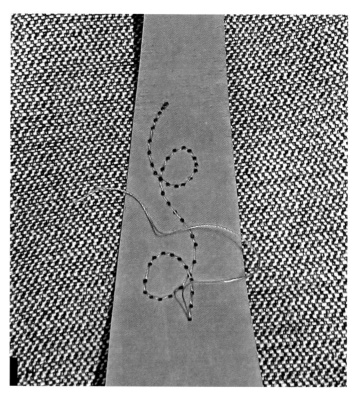

Photos on this page by Jenny K. Lyon

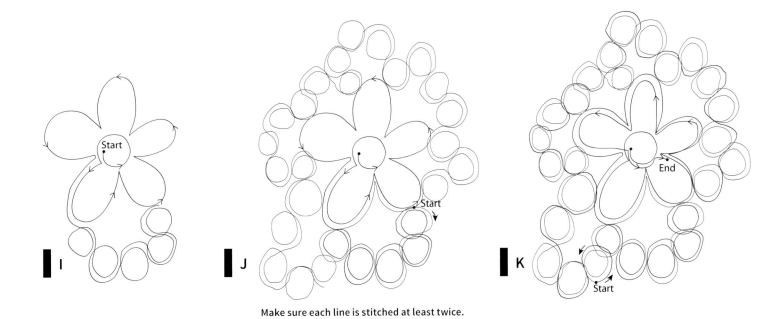

Make sure each line is stitched at least twice.

Quilt the Jacket

1. Begin to free-motion quilt the panel by starting with a daisy. You will be free-motion stitching the daisies without a drawn pattern, quilting each line twice. These are whimsical daisies like you drew in kindergarten. Don't count the petals; let them be a wee bit lopsided. This is not an exacting pattern—have fun with it!

Once you have finished one daisy, travel over the previous stitching line to the tip of one of the petals and begin to stitch enough Bubbles to reach the next daisy as shown in Prepare to Quilt, Step 2 (page 66).

Perfect stitching is not important here because the jacket has a Bohemian look. What is important is to leave enough space between motifs for the cutwork to show. I suggest leaving 1–3 finger widths of space between motifs. This will give you an open lacy look. Overfilling the space will result in an undefined blob of space. Better to leave too much space than not enough.

CHECK AS YOU GO

If you're not feeling confident that you have enough open space, stop after quilting about one-third of the panel and cut out the negative space. How does it look with the spaces cut out? You can self-correct based on how it looks. Is there enough space between the motifs? If not, you can add more space on the remaining part of the jacket.

2. Continue on in this manner, filling in the space. It's okay to stop the stitching line and start again in another area if you're not able to continuously stitch the line. As you stitch, free-motion quilt over each design line twice to secure the stitch line.

Cut the Negative Space

1. Now the cutwork begins! You might want to put on some sort of entertainment—books on tape, radio, favorite music, or light-hearted TV programming—for this part. Begin by taking a snip into the center part of each negative space, cutting only the denim material, *not* the kraft-tex underneath. Be mindful of where you are cutting. You do not want to cut into the design areas; you want to cut into the space between the design lines—the negative space. *Fig. A*

2. Once you have made the initial cuts, begin cutting each space. Place the tip of the bottom scissor blade underneath the denim and begin to cut. It is exciting to see the design begin to emerge! *Fig. B*

CUTTING TIPS

- It is more efficient if you hold the jacket firmly in your nondominant hand and move only your dominant hand with the scissors to cut into the nooks and crannies of the cutwork.

- It is easier if you make cuts in several areas all in one direction. Then rotate the jacket a quarter turn and make those cuts. You have to move the jacket less frequently that way.

- Slide the blade of the scissors over, not into, the surface of the kraft-tex and there will be no chance of cutting into it.

3. Once you have all the cutwork done, you can wash it as you would any other garment. After the first washing you will need to go back and clip off errant threads. *Fig. C*

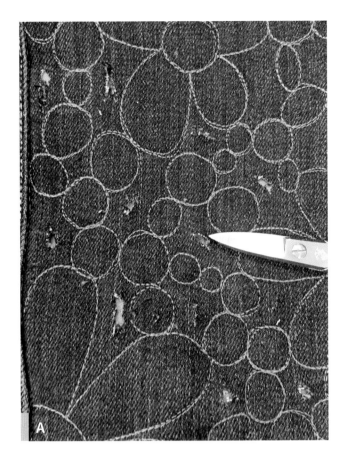

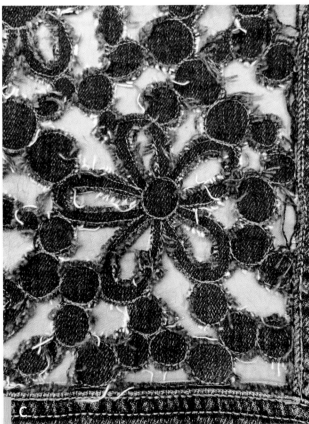

Stitch inside and cut out some of the petals if you prefer.

This same concept can be used with your own design. I used a filigree type of motif as my design for this jacket. I like it too!

Photos A–C by Jenny K. Lyon

STEP 3: Your Personal Quilting World

> For me, one of *the* most important and enjoyable parts of quilting are the friendships I have built with other quilters. Our friendships go far beyond quilting, and we are there to support and uplift each other.

I love that about quilting, and *Stars 'n' Stripes* was all about my friends and their support. It started out with a simple Mission Statement: This quilt was to be simple and fun, filled with feathers, which I adore, and it was to use some orphaned blocks.

My first task was to figure out how to unify all the different colored blocks. My friend Laura is very good with color. We went on a shopping mission and found the perfect color for the sashing.

I was about to begin piecing the top together when my friend Helen suggested some sort of frame for each block. She scoured the shop we were in and found that fabulous striped fabric. I was taken aback; I couldn't imagine that fabric as my frame! But once it was pieced in,

Stars 'n' Stripes, 46˝ × 46˝, 2012

I saw that it brought life to the quilt. With the help of my friends this quilt went from pretty to special!

Quilting friendships are part of a concept I am passionate about. That concept is that you build your own quilting world. No matter what the rest of your world is like, this corner of your world in which you quilt is under *your* control! You get to make all the choices—how liberating!

Bend, Don't Break, 21″ × 14″, 2012

> This quilt was made during a period of great challenges that threatened to overwhelm me. The process of designing and making *Bend, Don't Break* helped me make sense of a difficult time. I thought I was just doodling a quilt, but as the design progressed, I realized I was portraying my life at the time. Quilting can be healing.

The beauty about your own quilting world is that you can build it to suit your taste, time, budget, and desires. Perhaps your friends are into hand appliqué, and you're not. That's fine—build your own quilting world without hand appliqué.

Maybe you've got a stash of brightly colored fabrics. But the modern quilt movement wooed you and now you are looking for low-volume fabrics. It's your choice.

This quilting thing that we do is a passion. We build our passion decision by decision. Over time I have thoughtfully acquired the machine, set-up, and stash to suit my needs. I let go of some beautiful fabric and prime notions that no longer suit my needs.

I do this with no guilt—someone else loved those fabrics and notions! Over time my interests naturally distilled into the work I do now. It's a joy to walk into my studio and be surrounded by what I love, what I am passionate about.

It is my hope that you will purposefully build your own quilting world where you thrive and find joy.

Find Joy in All Your Work

When I first began to quilt, there were entire parts of the process that I didn't like, such as cutting and binding. I quickly realized that every quilt would have those parts.

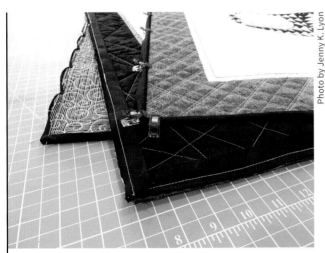

Photo by Jenny K. Lyon

I began to embrace and even enjoy the task of hand stitching my bindings.

I chose instead to consciously embrace those tasks. For example, I put on my favorite music when I was cutting fabric—what a difference that made! As I applied my binding, I reveled in the thought of a completed quilt.

Over time my thought process shifted, and I began to enjoy the entire process of quiltmaking. Each part became joyful, necessary for the beauty of the finished piece. Quilting then moved from being somewhat fun to being a joy-filled experience!

Mistakes

Mistakes are an important part of the quilting process, something to accept, even embrace. We learn from our mistakes! It is my hope that you will accept your mistakes first, and then decide what to do about them.

I don't automatically correct all of the mistakes I see. When I discover a mistake, in my mind's eye, I see a decision point. My rule is this: If I feel like the whole feeling of the quilt is wrong, I will fix it. That might include wrong thread color, wrong scale of quilting, wrong motif, or wrong thread entirely.

I envisioned this as the perfect motif and thread for *Summer Stars* (page 57). When I got to this point I realized it had to be fixed. The thread showed up surprisingly dark and the curved motif distracted from the stars. It was time to unstitch!

Lily Sample, 14″ × 14″, 2015

Some mistakes should be fixed. *Lily Sample* is a great example. I made this piece to experiment with the lily-of-the-valley motif. The scale of the lily and its surrounding fill were similar, making it difficult to discern the focal point of the quilt. If it had been a competition quilt, I would have ripped out the surrounding fill and chosen one with a smaller scale.

But I also know that I don't learn anything from ripping out stitching. Many times, my decision is to acknowledge my mistake and think about correcting that on the *next* quilt.

My motto is "Onward!," and most times I will accept my mistake and move on. I'm more interested in moving forward than in perfect quilts!

Be a Joiner

Joining a local guild or group will put you in touch with like-minded people who will encourage your growth and inspire you. Most guilds bring in speakers several times a year. I find that I learn something from every speaker, even if they are way outside of my genre.

I am currently active in four groups, and the camaraderie and support from these groups is special to me. They are there for technical support, yes, but also we support each other through life's highs and lows.

The longer I quilt, the more I am convinced that many of us quilt for the companionship. Quilting is so much more fun when you have friends to share your passion with! Most guilds also do significant charity work. What a rewarding experience to make a quilt for someone in need! Can you imagine if you were in the hospital and someone brought you a quilt? You can share in that joy through a guild.

I unexpectedly ran into members of my guild at a show. You will find like-minded friends in a guild.

JOIN OTHERS TO TAKE THE CHALLENGE

In 2016 I taught two workshops for the guild African-American Quilters of Los Angeles. What enthusiastic students they were! I later learned that they formed a group in response to my suggestion of 21 Days of Free-Motion Quilting (21FMQ). I was so excited to hear this!

Eight members decided to take the 21FMQ as a challenge. They each placticed (page 30) at home, but kept in touch with each other about their progress. Each member approached it differently: Some placticed on sandwiches, some on charity quilts, some finished quilts for their upcoming show. But all said that being part of the group was a valuable step in improving their skills.

These friends banded together to improve their skills and support each other. It is my strong belief that the support I've received from the guilds I am a part of has helped me become who I am today. I encourage *you* to also join with others on your free-motion quilting journey.

Members of the African-American Quilters of Los Angeles free-motion quilting group who took the 21FMQ challenge

Photos on this page by Jenny K. Lyon

Show Your Work

I know some of you cringe over the thought of showing your work. I hear the objection, "But my work isn't good enough to share." Yes, it is!

I attended many local quilt guild shows when I first began to quilt. I was awestruck at the incredible beauty of the quilts. The thought that I could ever achieve such artistry was ludicrous. And yet some of the more simple quilts inspired me; I thought, maybe *I* actually *could* do this!

Some viewers *need* to see more everyday quilts, something beautiful that they think they might be able to make. Even if your quilts are not the best in the show, you may have inspired a newer quilter to join in and quilt.

Besides the "show" factor, sharing your quilts is encouraging. You see how your quilt "plays" with others as it hangs among many. You see details in a new way—how the thread affects the quilt, how the batting choice compares, how the quilt hangs, and where the quilt stands among others for color and visual impact. All those elements have new meaning for you now because you have seen your quilt on display with others.

Each person will view your quilt differently, so share the beauty with others.

I encourage you to show that beauty to the world. We all need to see more beauty in our day!

Photos on this page by Jenny K. Lyon

Get Judged

There is much misunderstanding about having your work judged. Not everyone will want to have their work judged, but I encourage it. You can learn much from the experience.

This was my first judged item, and it was not a very encouraging experience!

My first experience having my work judged was horrible! I was new to quilting and entered the Wearable Art contest in my local guild. My guild was flush with internationally famous wearable artists, but that did not faze me. I entered this jacket into the contest. I was proud of my work and thought it was fabulous.

The judge did not.

She rated me poorly in all areas. I was stunned, then hurt. Then, I was motivated. I knew that judging was not supposed to be discouraging, and I set out to improve my work. I took classes, studied, and asked questions of the more experienced members of our guild. Two years later, I won a ribbon in Wearables in a major international show.

Every time I have had my work judged I have learned from the judge's comments. I did not always agree with them, but I learned how others might perceive my work.

Gallery of Quilts

My quilting has evolved since I made my first machine-quilted quilt in 1999 when I moved to California. I made exactly seven traditional quilts and then discovered that my favorite part of the process was the quilting. My love of the line and shadow created by the quilted stitch led me to the wholecloth quilts that I adore.

I usually start out with some sort of basic idea for my quilt, but many times the final piece is much different from the original idea. I sketch first and then experiment with thread and motifs on preliminary quilt sandwiches. I rarely go right to work on a quilt.

I now create primarily art quilts, and I particularly enjoy expressing what resonates in my soul upon a quilt. I gravitated toward the black-and-white format so that the viewer could see my design from afar. I try to make the backs of my quilts as interesting as the front, which surprises many a viewer.

I also learned what *not* do: I purchased the dupioni fabric on discount and never noticed the fade marks down the center until it was finished. I also pieced the back horizontally, which resulted in numerous tucks on the back.

If Diane Met Karen, silk dupioni and silk brocade, silk thread, wool batting, 46˝ × 63˝, 2006

This was a breakthrough quilt for me, when I fell in love with free-motion quilting and wholecloth quilts. I received four ribbons at my local guild's show! I was inspired by the work of Diane Gaudynski and Karen McTavish, hence the name.

Golden Moments, vintage hanky, Radiance fabric, silk and cotton threads, double batted with Orient and wool, 44˝ × 44˝, 2010

The vintage hanky in the middle provoked a strong memory of walking my boys to elementary school when we lived in northern New Jersey. It was a precious moment in time.

I chose to use mostly original motifs. The leaf motif in the middle required a lot of traveling and backtracking, a first for me. I started out marking each motif in the gray border and quickly realized I was perfectly happy with the little bit of wobble that comes from free-hand quilting without marks.

I created this garment for the summer days that may exceed 100 degrees here in the Sacramento Valley. I can pair this with a camisole and be cool yet covered up. It is a wonderful travel companion as it can be smashed in a suitcase and yet emerge without a wrinkle. It is one of my favorite garments.

I wanted to take the technique a little further after this vest and the Boho Cutwork Denim Jacket (page 62) takes the same technique but adds a layer of kraft-tex beneath the cutwork.

Daisy Vest, Italian cotton fused together, polyester thread, 2011

I had long wanted to quilt a garment and then cut out the negative space between motifs to create a lacy-looking garment. Daisy Vest was the first time I tried this technique, and I was hooked! The Italian denim I chose is a delight—it drapes beautifully on the body and has a lovely sheen, and the Mistyfuse did not add any stiffness.

Mom's Lily Bed, Radiance fabric, hand-dyed raw silk, silk dupioni, various threads, seed beads, wool batting, 52″ × 52″, 2012

I have a strong memory of sitting among a bed of ferns and lily-of-the-valley as a child. The smell was glorious and I shared my space with insects and butterflies. I had a few catastrophes along the way with this quilt. This is the first true wholecloth quilt that I designed from scratch, which was an act of faith. I was horrified to discover that the teal dupioni insert had bled, and I quickly learned how to fix a bleed. I used a wide variety of threads, and each one required that I experiment to find the best tension.

Emerge, cotton ombré fabric, polyester organza, variety of threads, wool batting, 20˝ × 26˝, 2012

I created a doodle for an online class in quilt design. I used the doodle as my inspiration for this quilt. The most challenging part was making thread choices that allowed the design to shine yet worked cohesively together. A good bit of unsewing made that happen! Tension was a bit tricky with the traditional quilt sandwich atop two layers of fused organza. I used Mistyfuse to fuse the organza together, and thankfully, it was stiff enough to be able to quilt the Bubbles without distortion or hooping.

Morning Breeze, cotton sateen, cotton and silk thread, wool batting, 49˝ × 57˝, 2013

This quilt is an interpretation of the beautiful landscaping in my Northern California yard, and it presented many challenges for me. I had to figure out how to represent my plants and trees by simplifying their shapes. I chose a very challenging thread combination, which required an extreme focus on tension; I used black 50-weight thread for the plantings and 100-weight silk thread for the bobbin. I also wanted to improve my skills of morphing from one motif to another in the background. Once completed, blocking the quilt to hang straight was yet another challenge due to the uneven density of the quilting.

Photo by RCP Scanning Services

Back of *Morning Breeze*. I made this quilt to be two-sided, and the back is my favorite! I adore the sheen of the silk thread and the way the entire surface is evenly covered with design.

Oat Grass, cotton sateen, silk, metallic and cotton thread, seed beads, wool batting, 11″ × 17″, 2013

I worked from a photo of my oat grass in the rain to capture its elegant beauty. I sketched the scene before committing to quilting it freehand on the quilt. I chose a simple facing for the edges instead of a binding.

Photo by Jenny K. Lyon

Breeze II, cotton sateen, cotton and silk thread, wool batting, 24″ × 18″, 2014

Breeze II is a spin-off from *Morning Breeze* (page 80). I took one of my favorite motifs from *Morning Breeze* and developed it into its own quilt. I studied my grasses carefully to come up with the design. I had to really hone my blocking skills, as there were areas of light quilting surrounded by heavy quilting. I was pleased with its elegant and spare design.

Back Story, hand-dyed wool, hand-dyed silk organza, polyester thread, 18″ × 25″, 2015

The glorious hand-dyed wool was my starting point. I am intrigued by the patterns of filigree, so I sketched until I found a design that pleased me. I auditioned a variety of threads, and I was surprised and pleased by the effect of the fluorescent orange thread. I don't normally work with polyester thread top and bobbin, so tension was a challenge. This is the same cutwork technique used on both Boho Cutwork Denim Jacket (page 62) and Daisy Vest (page 77).

Back of *Back Story*. Once quilted, the back became its own story, hence the name.

Prairie Conversation, cotton sateen, cotton and silk thread, wool batting, 45″ × 28″, 2015

> My inspiration came from a quick photo I took of the roadside weeds during a trip to my childhood home in North Central Illinois. I loved the way the photo captured the sense of movement and beauty of the weeds.

I greatly simplified the photo, including only the plants that were most interesting. I tried to quilt it without marking, but I wasn't capturing the movement of the grasses, so I added some markings with the help of a lightbox. I also simplified the quilting of the background by quilting it first, then the plants. Good tension between the thicker cotton and thin silk thread was an issue.

The black overlay was a late design decision. I had to make the quilt certain dimensions in order to enter it into a Studio Art Quilt Associates exhibit, so I created an entire white background in the dimensions I needed and added the first piece on top.

The Quiet Beauty of Imperfection (QBI), cotton sateen, silk thread, wool batting, 45″ × 54″, 2015

QBI is somewhat of a statement. I adore a beautifully executed imperfect quilt! There is beauty in perfection, but also beauty in imperfection. I chose to quilt this entire quilt without the use of rulers. I did mark some lines, but no rulers were used to quilt it. My lines wobble, which I find delightful.

I was inspired by the work of Yoshiko Jinzenji, known as the master of minimalism. My quilt is loosely based on the traditional pieced quilt block. Each quilted block is unique. My favorite part is the border, which I designed as I quilted.

Helen's Modern Circles, cotton solids, cotton and silk thread, wool batting, 51″ × 56″, designed and pieced by Helen Hardwick, 2015

I needed a quilt to illustrate modern quilting motifs for classes I was teaching at the Houston International Quilt Festival. Time was short, so I asked my friend Helen to design and piece the top with inset circles.

I had great fun deciding what motifs to use and where. I chose to morph from one motif to another in the gray and white areas. I did not use rulers on this quilt, and I learned that sometimes you do need to use them—learning curves sometimes show up in your work!

Photo by RCP Scanning Services

Stipa Gigantea, cotton sateen, cotton and silk thread, wool batting, 48˝ × 30˝, 2016

My favorite grass in my garden is the *Stipa gigantea*. I plucked a seed head, made a photocopy of it, and was shocked with the beauty of the design. I quilted the entire background and then added the grass head. This is one of my favorite pieces—I love the elegant beauty of a simple grass head.

Y 92, silk dupioni, cotton solids, polyester and cotton thread, wool batting, 18″ × 26″, 2016

Y 92 was created as part of a challenge organized by Pokey Bolton to honor the life of the iconic Yvonne Porcella. I did not know Yvonne personally, but I was greatly influenced by her work and the organization she founded, Studio Art Quilt Associates.

Now Quilt That Quilt

It is my hope you are confident enough to begin quilting those "special" quilts, the ones that you've been waiting to quilt "until you are good enough." If you have placticed (page 30) for 21 days and completed a few projects, you are ready. You are over the hump!

I send you on your free-motion quilting journey with a few suggestions as you fearlessly begin to tackle those challenging projects.

- Approach each project with joy! Every day that you quilt you get a little bit better.

- Make mindful choices as you go about your machine and quilting set-up.

- If there is a motif or area that is particularly challenging, draw it out on paper until you are proficient, then plactice on a few sandwiches until you are confident.

- Step back occasionally to view your quilt as you would when it's finished. Remember the Six-Foot Rule (page 31)!

- Don't aim for perfection; embrace "the hand of the maker." Your work will be so much more interesting!

Maine Girl, 12˝ × 12˝, 2014

I *know* that you can successfully free-motion quilt your own quilts. I hope you persevere until your quilts express what is in your heart. It is such a wonderful thing to share the beauty of a quilt with the world.

Onward!

Appendix of Quilting Motifs

Stipple

Loops

Random Echo

Square Stipple

Bubbles

Asterisk

Half-Moon

Daisies

Hook and Curve

Snail Trail

Branch

Start
Shell Border

Echoed Ribbon Border

Peacock

Ribbon Candy

Flutter

Start
Water

Start
S-Curve Border

Start

Geranium

Fern

Bubble Divider

Leaf and Curl

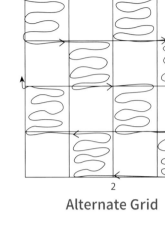
Alternate Grid

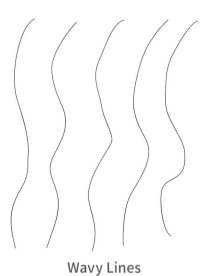
Wavy Lines

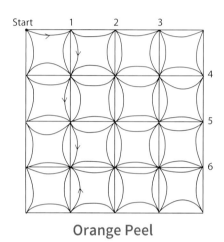
Orange Peel

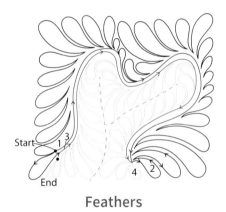
Feathers

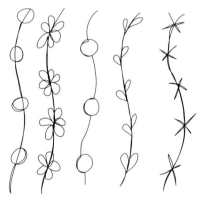
Various Wavy Lines with Motifs

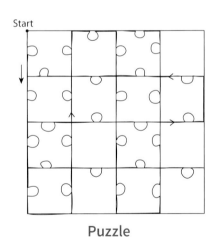
Puzzle

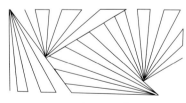
Margo's Border

About the Author

Jenny Lyon is a textile artist, author, lecturer, and teacher. She was born and raised in north central Illinois, learning to sew at age six. Although her mother and grandmother were quilters, the most important lesson she learned from them was, "If you want it, figure out how to make it."

Jenny's passion is teaching others to free-motion quilt, and she loves to meet new people as she travels to guilds, shops, and events throughout the United States. Her classes are personal, hands-on, and encouraging, and she believes anyone who desires can free-motion quilt.

Jenny enjoys sharing her work with the world through magazine articles, shows, and exhibitions and is featured on several *Quilting Arts TV* episodes as well as *The Quilt Show* with Alex Anderson and Ricky Tims. She wrote this book to encourage others to find their personal style of free-motion quilting.

Jenny lives in Northern California with her patient husband and an adorable Basset Boy. Their sons have left the nest, which leaves more room for her studio, fabric, and just a few sewing machines.

Follow Jenny online!

Blog: quiltskipper.com

Instagram: @jenny_quiltskipper

Pinterest: /quiltskipper

Facebook: /jenny.lyon.12

Want even more creative content?

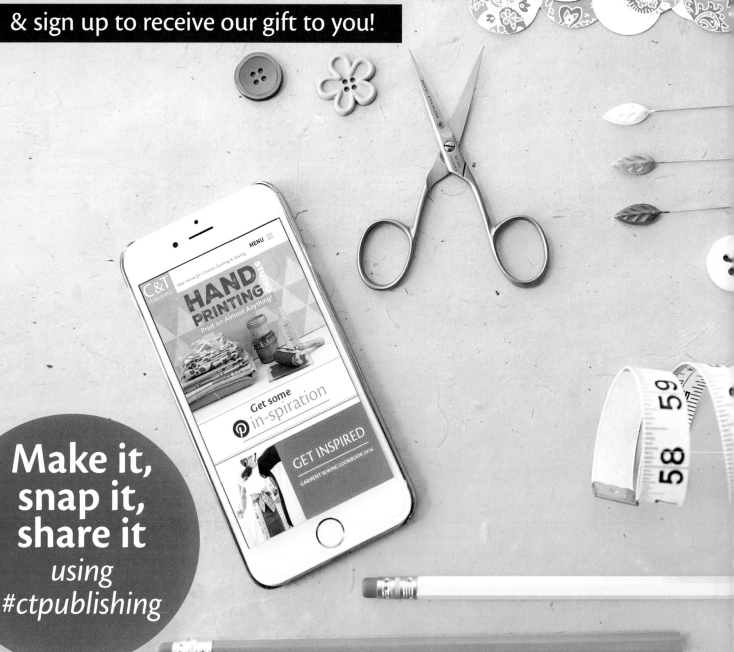

Make it, snap it, share it *using #ctpublishing*